PREVENTING CHALLENGING BEHAVIOR
in Your Classroom

Revised with an eye toward the ever-evolving research base undergirding positive behavior support (PBS) and related approaches, *Preventing Challenging Behavior in Your Classroom*, second edition, focuses on real-world examples and practical strategies to prevent and reduce behavior problems and enhance student learning.

Featuring a new chapter on culturally responsive PBS, this second edition helps readers understand disparities in punitive responses and identify strategies to promote equitable, positive school discipline. Teachers will be able to smartly appraise the efficacy of a range of classroom management practices with the help of updated standards, function-based strategies to differentiate evidence-based from questionable or harmful practices, and resources and tools for evaluation.

Written in engaging, easy-to-understand language, this book is an invaluable resource for pre- and in-service educators looking to strengthen their understanding and implementation of equitable PBS.

Matt Tincani is a Professor in the Department of Teaching and Learning at Temple University, USA. He focuses on the application of behavioral principles to improve language, academic, social, and play skills of learners with autism spectrum disorders and other disabilities, with a particular interest in Skinner's analysis of verbal behavior.

PREVENTING CHALLENGING BEHAVIOR

in Your Classroom

Classroom Management and Positive Behavior Support

Second Edition

Matt Tincani

Routledge
Taylor & Francis Group

NEW YORK AND LONDON

Cover image: Shutterstock

First published 2022
by Routledge
605 Third Avenue, New York, NY 10158

and by Routledge
2 Park Square, Milton Park, Abingdon, Oxon, OX14 4RN

Routledge is an imprint of the Taylor & Francis Group, an informa business

Library of Congress Cataloging-in-Publication Data
Names: Tincani, Matt, author.
Title: Preventing challenging behavior in your classroom: classroom management and positive behavior support/Matt Tincani.
Description: Second Edition. | New York: Routledge, 2022. | First edition: 2011. | Includes bibliographical references. |
Identifiers: LCCN 2021047441 (print) | LCCN 2021047442 (ebook) |
ISBN 9781032145013 (Hardback) | ISBN 9781646322053 (Paperback) |
ISBN 9781003237228 (eBook)
Subjects: LCSH: Classroom management. | Problem children–Behavior modification.
Classification: LCC LB3013 .T585 2022 (print) | LCC LB3013 (ebook) |
DDC 371.102/4–dc23/eng/20220125
LC record available at https://lccn.loc.gov/2021047441
LC ebook record available at https://lccn.loc.gov/2021047442

ISBN: 9781032145013 (hbk)
ISBN: 9781646322053 (pbk)
ISBN: 9781003237228 (ebk)

DOI: 10.4324/9781003237228

Typeset in Warnock Pro
by Deanta Global Publishing Services, Chennai, India

This book is dedicated to teachers with the courage to apply evidence-based practice in their classrooms.

Contents

Figures

Tables

Introduction

Virtually all teachers will encounter students who display problem behaviors in their classrooms. Positive behavior support (PBS) has evolved as the preeminent, research-based approach to help students with challenging behaviors to succeed in classroom settings. Educators across the country are embracing PBS as their primary means for student discipline, and a working knowledge of PBS is essential for classroom teachers to fully meet their students' learning, behavioral, and social needs, and to fulfill requirements of state and federal mandates.

Preventing Challenging Behavior in Your Classroom: Classroom Management and Positive Behavior Support targets regular and special education teachers who implement PBS in their classrooms. The book also serves as an essential resource for preservice teachers who are developing their classroom management skills. It focuses on practical strategies to prevent and reduce behavior problems and enhance student learning. The second edition of the book includes updated research, a new chapter on culturally responsive PBS, and expanded descriptions of classroom-level and individualized PBS interventions, with new examples and forms to accompany strategies presented in the book.

Initial chapters overview the conceptual and empirical basis of PBS; however, much of the book describes PBS for inclusive settings, including culturally responsive techniques for students with and without disabilities.

PBS interventions from peer-reviewed research are highlighted in easy-to-understand language to facilitate teachers' knowledge of evidence-based techniques. Real-world examples are provided in conjunction with activities to enhance teachers' understanding and mastery of the book's content.

Chapter 1, What Is Positive Behavior Support?, presents a brief history and overview of PBS, including primary, secondary, and tertiary levels of prevention. The chapter provides a context for the book's focus on classroom-level interventions.

Chapter 2, Culturally Responsive PBS, overviews how teachers can actively incorporate culturally responsive practice into their PBS strategies.

Chapter 3, Myths and Facts About Effective Classroom Management, describes common misconceptions about classroom management, setting the stage for a discussion of effective interventions.

Chapter 4, The Foundation: Classroom Organization, discusses the keys to good classroom organization with real-world examples of organizational techniques.

Chapter 5, Active Student Responding to Prevent Challenging Behaviors, presents instructional techniques that encourage active student responding to reduce challenging behavior in the classroom. Strategies covered in this chapter include response cards, choral responding, guided notes, and brisk instructional pacing.

Chapter 6, Classroom-Wide Behavior Support, outlines basic principles of behavior and targeted strategies for students at risk for academic failure due to behavior problems.

Chapter 7, Functional Behavioral Assessment, targets students with chronic challenging behaviors. The chapter describes why students engage in problem behaviors and presents a continuum of strategies to assess behavior functions.

Chapter 8, Function-Based Interventions and Behavior Intervention Programming, discusses strategies for individualized interventions, with an emphasis on function-based supports and behavior intervention program development.

Chapter 9, Using Data to Evaluate PBS Outcomes, overviews the role of data in program evaluation, with techniques to collect and evaluate student data.

Chapter 10, Putting It Together: Evidence-Based Classroom Management Inventory, presents one strategy for assessing and improving the teacher's implementation of effective classroom management techniques.

Each chapter begins with a set of chapter objectives. The reader should overview each objective to understand what they are expected to learn. Each chapter also contains a set of guided activities embedded throughout the text.

It is useful to complete these activities while reading the text to enhance understanding of the chapters' content. Finally, Chapter 10 contains the Reflective Classroom Manager Survey, which is designed to help in-service teachers reflect on their use of techniques described in the book and develop an action plan for improving key strategies.

CHAPTER 1

What Is Positive Behavior Support?

Chapter Objectives

- Describe the history of positive behavior support (PBS)

- Understand how PBS is part of the Individualized Educational Program process in special education

- Describe the three levels of PBS intervention

- Understand how PBS is an example of Evidence-Based Practice

- Identify similarities and differences between PBS and Response to Intervention and how both are Multi-Tiered Systems of Support

DOI: 10.4324/9781003237228-1

In this chapter, we will overview the history of positive behavior support (PBS) and its role within special education and behavior intervention programming. We will identify the critical features of PBS and explore school-based applications of each critical feature. Then, we will learn about primary, secondary, and tertiary prevention as core elements of PBS in schools, as implemented in School-Wide Positive Behavioral Interventions and Supports (SWPBIS). We will conclude with a discussion of similarities and differences between SWPBIS and response to intervention (RTI) as multi-tiered systems of support (MTSS).

Ms. Ramirez's New Class

Ms. Ramirez is excited to begin her first year of teaching. She recently completed a teacher preparation program at a local university and has secured a position in an inclusive elementary school classroom. She is eager to organize her room, plan her lessons, and meet her students, but she is anxious about the challenges her first year of teaching will present. After reviewing her new students' individualized educational programs (IEPs), she realizes that several of them have behavior intervention programs (BIPs) to reduce problem behaviors. Furthermore, the students' BIPs include an unfamiliar term, Positive Behavior Support. With this new information in mind, she wonders how she can best enable all of her students to be successful in school, including her students with challenging behavior.

What Is Positive Behavior Support?

Positive Behavior Support and the IEP

As Ms. Ramirez's vignette illustrates, there is a lot of information for new teachers to learn. For instance, all students with disabilities who receive special education services have an IEP that describes their annual goals and short-term objectives, how their educational progress will be measured, and what accommodations and related services they will receive, in addition to other important information (Individuals with Disabilities Education Improvement Act of 2004, H.R. 1350, Sec. 614 (d)(1)(A)(i)). In essence, the IEP describes how a student's special education program will be delivered and the manner in which the student's educational progress will be evaluated.

Some students with disabilities engage in challenging behaviors. These behaviors make it difficult for students to benefit from instruction and may create a distracting environment for others around them. For children with disabilities who engage in challenging behaviors that interfere with learning, the IEP team must consider strategies, including PBS, to minimize those behaviors. Specifically, when developing an IEP, the team must:

> In the case of a child whose behavior impedes the child's learning or that of others, consider the use of *positive behavioral interventions and supports*, and other strategies, to address that behavior.
> (Individuals with Disabilities Education Improvement Act of 2004, H.R. 1350, Sec. 300.324(a) (2)(i))

So, as members of the educational team — special education teachers, regular education teachers, parents, school psychologists, administrators, and others — develop an IEP for a student with challenging behaviors, it is critical for them to consider PBS. PBS intervention strategies may be described within a BIP, a written plan that describes procedures to prevent and reduce a student's challenging behaviors. We will learn more about BIPs in Chapter 8.

Positive Behavior Support and Effective Classroom Management

But there is much more to PBS than developing BIPs for students with behavior problems. As we will see, PBS includes a variety of strategies to help teachers effectively manage their classrooms to

Behavior intervention plan (BIP): A written plan that describes procedures to prevent and reduce a student's challenging behaviors, and how data will be used to evaluate these procedures. BIPs are designed for students who display chronic or intense challenging behaviors.

Individualized education program (IEP): A written plan that describes how a student's special education program will be delivered and evaluated. Required components include present levels of performance, measurable goals and objectives, related services and accommodations, and how the child's progress will be documented.

Positive behavior support (PBS): An approach to prevent and reduce challenging behavior through comprehensive lifestyle change, a lifespan perspective, stakeholder participation, socially valid interventions, systems change, multicomponent intervention, prevention, flexibility with respect to scientific practices, and multiple theoretical perspectives.

promote student learning. In fact, a central component of PBS is arranging the student's environment to *prevent* challenging behaviors from occurring to begin with (Carr et al., 2002; Dunlap et al., 2018). With this in mind, we will discuss PBS as a comprehensive approach to prevent and reduce challenging behaviors and to enhance the overall success of students in school and quality of life.

Defining Positive Behavior Support

The importance of PBS to effective behavior intervention is clear; however, there is no simple, straightforward definition of PBS, nor is PBS associated exclusively with any particular set of teaching techniques. The best way to understand PBS is to examine its historical roots and define its features, as well as its applications within school settings.

PBS emerged over three decades ago as a movement to support the use of non-aversive behavior interventions for persons with disabilities (Horner et al., 1990). Until the 1990s, it was not uncommon for students to receive humiliating, painful, or physically harmful 'treatments' – including physical and chemical restraints – to reduce their problem behaviors. So, PBS emerged in part as a movement to discourage educators from using such aversive procedures. Although physical and chemical restraints are no longer considered acceptable practices, other punishment-based discipline procedures, such as suspension, are still commonly used in schools, with low-income and minority students disproportionately subjected to these practices (Cholewa et al., 2018). To discourage the use of aversive discipline practices and punishment in schools, we must offer effective alternatives. So, the founders of PBS were careful to extend its scope beyond the rejection of aversive interventions. They defined PBS to include a range of approaches that emphasized (a) effective, positive procedures; (b) social validation and human dignity; and (c) prohibition of certain aversive behavior change techniques, including those involving pain, harm, disrespect, or dehumanization of the individual (Horner et al., 1990, pp. 126–130). We will discuss specific reasons for avoiding punishment aversive behavior interventions in Chapter 3.

Importantly, the field of PBS has been heavily influenced by the science of applied behavior analysis (ABA) (Cooper et al., 2020) and shares much in common with it. For example, ABA and PBS emphasize data-based decision making, careful examination of the students' environment to understand why behaviors are occurring, and a practical, problem-solving approach to intervention (Dunlap et al., 2008). Indeed, many of the procedures described throughout this book come directly from the science of ABA (Cooper et al., 2020). Yet, there are several critical features of contemporary PBS that set it apart from ABA (Carr et al., 2002). The critical features are comprehensive lifestyle change and quality of life; a lifespan perspective; stakeholder participation; social validity; systems change and multicomponent intervention; emphasis on prevention; flexibility with respect to scientific practices; and multiple theoretical perspectives.

Applied behavior analysis (ABA): The application of the science of behavior analysis to improve socially significant behaviors. ABA emphasizes continuous measurement, close examination of the student's environment, and manipulation of antecedents and consequences to accomplish behavior change.

Critical Features of Positive Behavior Support

The critical features of PBS are summarized below. While each is distinct, you will notice overlap among them. We will refer to the critical features of PBS throughout the remaining chapters of the book as we discuss the applications of PBS in classroom management.

Comprehensive Lifestyle Change and Quality of life

The focus of intervention is not just the problem behavior itself, but how the problem behavior affects the student's lifestyle and quality of life.

Example: Joseph, a preschool student, often hits his classmates to access a toy he wants. Joseph's hitting is not only disruptive to the classroom, but his behavior has caused other students to avoid him, and he has formed few friendships with his peers. Joseph's hitting has negatively affected his quality of life by limiting his social relationships. If PBS is successful, Joseph will not only hit his peers less frequently, but he will also have more friendships with students in his class. We could measure this outcome by recording the frequency of appropriate, reciprocal peer interactions before and after intervention. Increased peer interactions would indicate that Joseph's quality of life has improved according to the dimension of friendships.

Lifespan Perspective

The intervention accomplishes both short- and long-term behavior change. Positive outcomes are measured not just in days and weeks, but in months and years.

Example: Elaine is a 16-year-old girl with intellectual disabilities. Upon finishing high school, she wants to secure competitive employment in the community. However, her occasional outbursts have prevented her from participating in her high school's work-study program. Therefore, a short-term goal of PBS for Elaine is inclusion in her high school's work-study program, and a long-term goal is attaining a full-time job when she graduates. Elaine's educational team will consider both her short- and long-term vocational goals when developing her PBS plan.

Stakeholder Participation

Stakeholders are actively involved in the design and implementation of behavior support programs. Stakeholders can include parents, grandparents, teachers, siblings, friends, or anyone who has a meaningful relationship with the focus person. Stakeholder participation in PBS is a key component of culturally responsive practice (Vincent et al., 2011). These strategies emphasize teachers' cultural knowledge and self-awareness, a commitment to supports that are relevant to their students' cultures and identities, and a focus on decision making to enhance culturally equitable outcomes (See Chapter 2). For instance, when students' family members are actively involved in the development of PBS strategies, the strategies are more likely to reflect the values of the student, their family, and their community. This results in the identification of culturally relevant target behaviors and intervention strategies, which are more likely to be supported by the student's family and accepted within the community.

Example: Di's educational team convenes to develop his PBS plan. The team is comprised not only of educators and Di's parents but also his grandparents and older sister. The team seeks input from each family member to identify routines in the home setting that are affected by his problem behavior. Family members help to select target behaviors and design interventions that will reduce his challenging behaviors across settings.

Social Validity

Interventions are evaluated not only in terms of objective data but also in terms of stakeholders' subjective perceptions of their utility and effectiveness (Schwartz & Baer, 1991). Team members seek active input from stakeholders on the goals of interventions, their feasibility, and how effective they are in producing desired outcomes.

Example: Julio's team implements a PBS plan to reduce his destructive and aggressive behaviors. As the plan is developed, Julio's teacher and teaching assistant are actively engaged by the team to ensure that they understand the plan and can implement it. The procedures are adjusted to meet their skills and preferences. After the plan is put in place, the team periodically evaluates staff satisfaction with the procedures and, importantly, whether they have continued to implement them. The teacher and teaching assistant are satisfied with the procedures and outcomes of Julio's PBS plan and have continued to implement the plan with fidelity.

Systems Change and Multicomponent Intervention

Long-term solutions rely upon changing environments that support problem behaviors, with careful attention to the people who implement PBS. No behavior reduction program will be successful unless stakeholders understand the procedures, are well trained, and have the resources to be successful. Because the environments in which students behave are complex, successful plans must have multiple procedures to address challenging behaviors.

Example: Rollins Middle School has a high rate of office discipline referrals, detentions, and suspensions among its students. To address students' chronic behavior problems, Rollins' staff implements a SWPBIS program (Horner & Sugai, 2015; Sugai & Horner, 2002), which is developed with input from the entire school staff. The program includes ongoing personnel training and data-based decision making targeting culturally equitable outcomes. Multiple interventions are developed at the school-wide, classroom, and individual student levels to address the discipline needs of all students.

Emphasis on Prevention

Well-designed behavior support plans prevent challenging behaviors. Therefore, behavior change procedures are in place when problem behaviors are not occurring, and school personnel adopt a proactive, skill-building approach to solving behavior problems.

Example: Emily is a middle-school student with autism. She often becomes confused and has tantrums during activity transitions. Recognizing the need to make Emily's transitions more concrete, her teacher implements a picture activity schedule to prevent tantrums. Once in place, Emily no longer becomes confused when activities end, and she has learned to become more independent as she transitions from one activity to the next.

Flexibility with Scientific Practices and Multiple Theoretical Perspectives

The practice of PBS reflects the influence of diverse scientific, theoretical, and professional perspectives. Team members recognize the role of the focus person's learning history, social systems, and cultural contexts as critical influences on his or her behavioral development. Team members value the perspectives of professionals from varying disciplines and the diverse perspectives they bring to bear on solutions to challenging behaviors.

Example: Naoki is a pre-K student with intellectual disabilities and challenging behaviors whose family recently emigrated from Japan. His PBS team carefully listens to his parents to understand their goals for intervention. They learn that Naoki spends much of his time with his mother and that his problem behaviors have made her and Naoki relatively isolated with few trips into the community. Therefore, the PBS team develops interventions that seek to reduce his problem behaviors within relevant community routines (e.g., grocery shopping, doctor's office). Similar interventions are applied in the school setting.

Adapted from Carr, E. G., Dunlap, G., Horner, R. H., Koegel, R. L., Turnbull, A. P., Sailor, W., et al. (2002). Positive behavior support: Evolution of an applied science. *Journal of Positive Behavior Interventions, 4*, 4–16, 20.

Positive Behavior Support versus Positive Behavioral Interventions and Supports

Any teacher new to the field will quickly realize there are many acronyms and terms used by educators. Though professionals use the term PBS to describe the concepts and procedures outlined in this book, you may also hear the term positive behavioral interventions and supports (PBIS) in reference to the same approaches (Sugai, & Simonsen, 2012). There is no fundamental difference between PBS and PBIS; both describe a continuum of strategies emphasizing the same non-aversive procedures with a heavy focus on systems, prevention, and data-based decision making. Whereas PBS originated in response to the use of aversive intervention strategies for people with disabilities, the term PBIS was later introduced to describe the application of PBS systems at the school-wide level (Dunlap et al., 2014), and has become synonymous with the school-wide applications described in the next section. Because the focus of this book is primarily classroom management and individual teacher strategies, we will use the term PBS throughout the book, unless we are discussing school-wide applications specifically.

Applying PBS in Schools: School-Wide Positive Behavior Interventions and Supports and the PBS Triangle

The critical features of PBS have been applied in over 25,000 schools within a model known as School-Wide Positive Behavioral Interventions and Supports (Horner & Sugai, 2015; OSEP Technical Assistance Center on PBIS, 2021; Sugai, 2007). SWPBIS uses a three-tiered model to address problem behaviors, with a focus on prevention, stakeholder participation, systems change, and multicomponent interventions. The three-tiered model has been depicted in the 'triangle' of PBS shown in Figure 1.1. As you can see, the triangle is composed of primary, secondary, and tertiary levels of prevention. Importantly, SWPBIS is a comprehensive approach that addresses students'

> SWPBIS is an application of PBS in schools that emphasizes systems of support at primary, secondary, and tertiary levels.

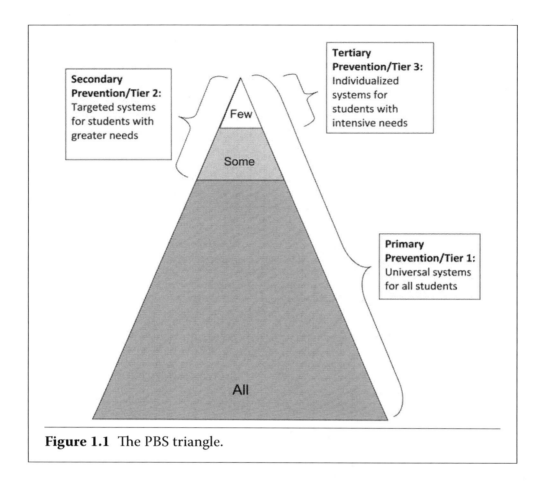

Figure 1.1 The PBS triangle.

behaviors differently based on their individual needs. Outcome data is used at all tiers of support to evaluate the effectiveness of SWPBIS procedures and adapt them, as needed, to promote successful, culturally equitable outcomes.

Primary Prevention

Primary prevention (also called Tier 1) focuses on all of the students in the school, the majority of whom require only this level of support. An important goal of these procedures is to prevent students who display low-level challenging behaviors from needing more intensive interventions. Primary prevention is comprised of universal interventions that are implemented in all school settings (e.g., classrooms, hallways, cafeteria, playground). Examples of universal interventions include school-wide rules and expectations, procedures for teaching rules and expectations, and a school-wide reward system.

Secondary Prevention

Secondary prevention (also called Tier 2) targets students who have greater behavioral needs and therefore benefit from targeted interventions. These students comprise a smaller portion of the school's population. One important reason for these strategies is to prevent students who display moderate levels of problem behaviors from needing intensive, individualized interventions. Secondary prevention consists of specialized group interventions, which are often implemented at the classroom level. Examples of secondary interventions include classroom-wide token reward systems, interventions for promoting active student responding, social skills training, and peer-mediated strategies. Examples of secondary interventions will be described in Chapters 5 and 6.

Tertiary Prevention

Tertiary prevention (also called Tier 3) focuses on students with the greatest needs, those with serious challenging behaviors that substantially interfere with their learning or the learning of others. The primary purpose of tertiary prevention is to reduce the effects of the student's problem behaviors on his or her academic, social, and behavioral success. Interventions at the tertiary level target only a few students relative to the entire school population. Often, these students receive special education services and/or require BIPs to address their problem behaviors. Tertiary interventions are intensive, individualized, and based on behavior function, that is, the antecedents and consequences that maintain problem responses. Examples of tertiary prevention are described in Chapter 8.

ACTIVITY

Consider a student you know who exhibits challenging behaviors or think of a hypothetical student who exhibits challenging behaviors. Based on what you just read, provide at least one example of primary, secondary, and tertiary interventions that would be appropriate to prevent and reduce the student's problem behaviors. These could be strategies that are already in place or new strategies.

- Primary prevention:

_____

_____

_____

_____

- Secondary prevention:

_____

_____

_____

_____

- Tertiary prevention:

_____

_____

_____

_____

PBS as Evidence-Based Practice

Slocum et al. (2014) define evidence-based practice (EBP) as a model of decision making that relies on 1) the best available research evidence, 2) consumer values and context, and 3) clinical expertise (Figure 1.2). An important distinction of Slocum et al.'s definition is that EBP is an active decision-making process that incorporates multiple intervention

> **Evidence-based practice (EBP)**: A model of decision making that relies on 1) the best available research evidence, 2) consumer values and context, and 3) clinical expertise.

strategies, rather than just one discrete intervention or practice. The best available research evidence comes from published and unpublished research studies, as well as systematic reviews of studies, that support intervention strategies. The greater the number of high-quality, rigorous research studies in support of a practice, the greater our confidence the practice will work (Cook & Odom, 2013). In some cases, there may be little current research to inform a solution for a specific problem. Thus, we must investigate how research has addressed similar problems, or otherwise rely more heavily on the other two components of EBP. Consumer values and context refer to how we incorporate the perspectives of students, families, and staff into the goals of PBS interventions, as well as our specific intervention strategies. This is an important aspect of social validity (Schwartz & Baer, 1991). Finally, clinical expertise describes

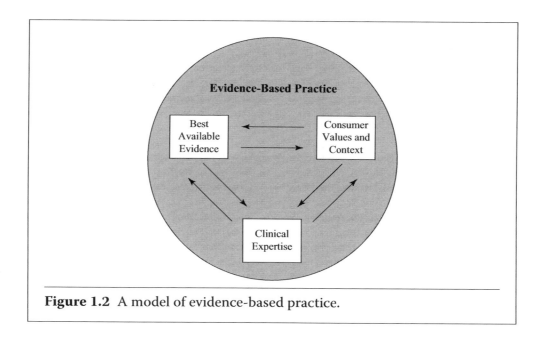

Figure 1.2 A model of evidence-based practice.

the knowledge, skills, experience, and training that teachers and school staff bring to bear in problem-solving situations.

As an approach to preventing challenging behavior, PBS aligns very closely with Slocum et al.'s (2014) definition of EBP. First, ample research supports the effectiveness of PBS in reducing challenging behavior across a variety of populations and settings (Goh & Bambara, 2012; Gage et al., 2018; Marquis et al., 2000). Second, with its emphasis on shared decision making, stakeholder participation, and outcome data, PBS implementers closely incorporate consumer values and context into their behavior support practices. Finally, ongoing staff training and professional development to promote implementers' clinical expertise have been identified as core features of sustained, high-quality PBS (Dunlap et al., 2000).

PBS and Response to Intervention

RTI is a related approach that has gained popularity and support in schools, school districts, and state departments of education throughout the United States (Arden et al., 2017). RTI and SWPBIS are both examples of multi-tiered systems of support (MTSS), in which students receive increasingly intensive levels of support based on need as determined by their responsiveness to intervention. RTI uses a multi-tiered prevention model to help students who are at-risk for academic difficulty because of learning problems, particularly in reading (Fuchs & Deshler, 2007; Fuchs & Fuchs, 2008). Like SWPBIS, RTI emphasizes prevention of academic failure through proactive strategies, focusing on the primary grades, when learning fundamental academic skills is most critical to later success. RTI focuses primarily on academic skills whereas SWPBIS mainly focuses on challenging behaviors. However, given the close interplay between behavioral success and academic outcomes (e.g., Gage et al., 2017), some schools, school districts, government agencies, and policy organizations may consider SWPBIS and RTI to be fundamentally similar and may describe both simply as MTSS.

Tier 1 of RTI is comprised of effective general education for all students to teach reading, math, and other fundamental academic skills. At Tier 1, all students are routinely screened for

Response to intervention (RTI): A multi-tiered approach that emphasizes prevention of academic failure through early screening and intervention.

Multi-tiered systems of support (MTSS): A model of service delivery in which students receive increasingly intensive levels of support based on their responsiveness to intervention.

the early signs of academic difficulties; those who are identified as 'non-responders' – that is, they do not display grade- or age-level proficiency with effective general education – are referred for more intensive interventions at Tier 2. Students who fail to respond to interventions at Tiers 1 and 2 may be evaluated for special education services and receive individual academic interventions at Tier 3. An important goal of RTI is to reduce the number of students who need special education services through early screening and early intervention (Bayat et al., 2010).

Summary

Positive Behavior Support emerged in the early 1990s as an alternative to aversive interventions for problem behaviors. Influenced strongly by the science of applied behavior analysis, contemporary PBS has evolved into a comprehensive approach to challenging behaviors that emphasizes the following: comprehensive lifestyle change and quality of life; a lifespan perspective; stakeholder participation; social validity; systems change and multicomponent intervention; emphasis on prevention; flexibility with respect to scientific practices; and multiple theoretical perspectives. PBS is embedded within IDEA '04; professionals must employ PBS strategies with students who have disabilities and display problem behaviors that interfere with their instruction or others' instruction. PBS has been widely implemented in an approach known as school-wide positive behavior interventions and supports, which is guided by three levels of prevention, primary, secondary, and tertiary. PBS aligns closely with EBP and has solid research support. RTI is a related approach that emphasizes the prevention of academic failure through a multi-tiered screening and intervention process. Both SWPBIS and RTI are multi-tiered systems of support, a model of service delivery in which students receive increasingly intensive levels of support based on their responsiveness to intervention.

Key Terms

Applied behavior analysis (ABA) – Application of the science of behavior analysis to improve socially significant behaviors. ABA emphasizes continuous measurement, close examination of the student's environment, and manipulation of antecedents and consequences to accomplish behavior change.

Behavior intervention program (BIP) – A written plan that describes procedures to prevent and reduce a student's challenging behaviors, and how data will be used to evaluate these procedures. BIPs are designed for students who display chronic or intense challenging behaviors.

Culturally response practice – Strategies that emphasize teachers' cultural knowledge and self-awareness, a commitment to supports that are relevant to their students' cultures and identities, and a focus on data-based decision making to enhance culturally equitable outcomes.

Evidence-based practice (EBP) – A model of decision making that relies on 1) the best available research evidence, 2) consumer values and context, and 3) clinical expertise.

Individualized educational program (IEP) – A written plan that describes how a student's special education program will be delivered. Required components include present levels of performance, measurable goals and objectives, related services and accommodations, and how the child's progress will be documented.

Multi-tiered systems of support (MTSS) – A model of service delivery in which students receive increasingly intensive levels of support based on their responsiveness to intervention.

Positive behavior support (PBS) – An approach to prevent and reduce challenging behavior through comprehensive lifestyle change, a lifespan perspective, stakeholder participation, socially valid interventions, systems change, multicomponent intervention, prevention, flexibility with respect to scientific practices, and multiple theoretical perspectives. Also known as Positive behavioral interventions and supports (PBIS).

Response to intervention (RTI) – A multi-tiered approach that emphasizes prevention of academic failure through early screening and intervention.

School-Wide Positive Behavioral Interventions and Supports (SWPBIS) – An application of PBS in schools that emphasizes systems of support at primary, secondary, and tertiary levels.

Additional Resources

To learn more about PBS, SWPBIS, and RTI, visit the following websites:

The Association for Positive Behavior Support: www.apbs.org

OSEP Technical Assistance Center on Positive Behavioral Interventions and Supports: www.pbis.org

National Center for Pyramid Model Innovations (NCPMI): www.challengingbehavior.org

RTI Network: www.rtinetwork.org

CHAPTER 2

Culturally Responsive PBS

Chapter Objectives

- Define culture.

- Explain the role culture plays in effective classroom management.

- Reflect on your own culture and how this affects your interactions with students.

- Identify key features of culturally responsive PBS.

- Understand the role of data to evaluate disparities in punitive school discipline.

- Identify strategies to promote equitable, positive school discipline.

DOI: 10.4324/9781003237228-2

In this chapter, we will overview the key elements of culturally responsive PBS. We will define culture and describe how culture affects our views and behavior, and our interactions with students. Then, we will explore the key features of culturally responsive PBS, an active approach that emphasizes diverse student, family, and community voices. We will conclude with a discussion of disproportionality in punitive school discipline, how we can use data to evaluate for disproportionality among diverse students, and data-based strategies for ensuring equitable school discipline.

What Is Culture?

Culture: The socially learned behaviors, values, preferences, and knowledge specific to a group of people.

Culture describes the socially learned behaviors, values, preferences, and knowledge specific to a group of people (Birukou et al., 2013). Each of us belongs to one or more unique cultures that have been transmitted to us by others, including our family members and the larger community. For example, nationality is an important aspect of culture, in that individuals who live in one country or region are more likely to adopt the language, food preferences, musical tastes, hobbies, and other social norms prevailing in that country or region. Importantly, some aspects of culture, such as nationality, come to us through circumstances beyond our control, whereas others are adopted through personal choices. For instance, a child raised in one religious tradition might choose a different religious tradition as an adult and adopt the cultural practices and beliefs of their new religion. Or they might adopt atheistic beliefs and choose not to adhere to the cultural practices of any religion or religious group.

Cultural diversity encompasses a wide variety of behaviors, values, preferences, and knowledge. Cultural diversity includes, but is not limited to, differences in sexual preference, sexual identity, race and ethnicity, language, political views, and religious or atheistic beliefs. Disability is also an important aspect of cultural diversity. For example, some people with autism spectrum disorder (ASD) do not view their autism as a disability, but as a normal variation of the human condition that brings unique strengths and positive qualities (Gillespie-Lynch et al., 2017). Accordingly, they may refer to themselves in identity-first language as an 'autistic person' rather than a 'person with autism' to reflect pride in their identity. Still, others may be comfortable referring to themselves as a 'person with autism,' and some might not wish to disclose their ASD to others. Ultimately, recognizing the value of cultural diversity involves understanding and respecting cultural differences, including how others' cultural preferences and values are different than your own.

How Is Culture Important in Classroom Management?

Culture is critical to effective classroom management and school discipline in several key ways. First, since all teachers come to the classroom with their own unique cultural identities, they must recognize how their own cultural perspectives impact their expectations of students and their interactions with

Cultural self-awareness: Understanding your own cultural perspectives, others' cultural perspectives, and how these affect your interactions.

them. A teacher raised in a culture where children are expected to speak to adults only when they are first spoken to may be surprised when, on the first day of school, her students speak freely to her without raising their hands. Initially, she might feel the urge to reprimand them for speaking out in this manner but recognizing their communication as an aspect of cultural difference, she might decide it is okay as long as it is not disruptive to the lesson. *Cultural self-awareness* involves understanding your own cultural perspectives, others' cultural perspectives, and how these affect your interactions. This level of self-awareness is important when you are teaching students whose culture is different than your own, as it creates a framework for understanding and successfully negotiating cultural differences with your students and their families (Rossetti et al., 2017). In reflecting on how your own culture is different from your students' culture, you may realize you know little about their cultural backgrounds. This may set the occasion for you to seek knowledge about their community's unique language, beliefs, and practices toward enhancing your own cultural awareness.

A second important way that culture affects classroom management is how it guides your lesson design and behavior support practices. Consider James, a first-year middle school math teacher who is teaching a class of mostly Latinx students for whom English is their second language. As he conducts a lesson on reducing fractions, he notices the students seldom raise their hands to answer his questions, are disengaged, and perform a variety of off-task behaviors. Upon reflection, he realizes their limited English proficiency is a barrier to their participation because he is relying on their spoken language to answer his questions about math. James decides to try a variation of this lesson using write-on response cards, where students write their answers on whiteboards and then simultaneously raise them to receive feedback (Tincani & Twyman, 2016; see Chapter 5). When students use write-on response cards, their participation and engagement in the lesson immediately increase, and they perform fewer off-task behaviors. This example shows how consideration of culture can lead to more effective instructional and behavior support practices in the classroom.

It is also apparent how culture affects classroom management when we examine data on the disproportionate impact of school-based discipline practices on racially and ethnically diverse students. Research in this area consistently shows that students from minority groups, including African American and Latinx students, are disproportionately subjected to punitive discipline practices, and these practices contribute to negative academic outcomes (Gregory et al., 2010; Morris & Perry, 2016; Sullivan et al., 2013). In this context, punitive discipline practices include in-school and out-of-school suspension, expulsion, and other forms of punishment. Fortunately, other research has shown that high fidelity application of PBS in schools can reduce disproportionality in punitive discipline while reducing the application of punitive discipline practices for all students (McIntosh et al., 2018). In this book, you will learn about evidence-based, positive strategies as alternatives to punishment-based discipline in helping all students succeed in school.

Considering Your Own Culture Awareness

Take a moment to reflect on yourself and the students you teach, or if you are not yet a teacher, the kinds of students you might encounter in your future role as a teacher. If you plan to teach in a specific geographic area, think about whether there are students from particular cultural groups that you are likely to teach. Write down your thoughts in response to the following questions:

1. What is your own cultural background? Consider your identity, your parents' identities, and your family background. What are examples of behaviors, values, preferences, and knowledge that are specific to your culture?

_____

_____

_____

_____

2. What are your students' cultural backgrounds and how do they differ from yours? How much do you know about their cultures and how could you learn more?

_____

_____

_____

_____

3. How does your students' culture affect their learning in the classroom? What are possible ways you can adapt your instruction to meet their linguistic and cultural needs?

_____

_____

_____

_____

Culturally Responsive PBS

Culturally responsive practice emphasizes teachers' cultural knowledge and self-awareness, a commitment to supports that are relevant to their students' cultures and identities, and a focus on data-based decision making to enhance culturally equitable outcomes (Vincent et al., 2011). Since the features of PBS emphasize stakeholder input, a focus on social validity, and data-based outcomes, cultural responsiveness is already built into key aspects of the PBS framework and approach. Throughout the remaining chapters, we will emphasize how specific PBS strategies align with culturally responsive practice. Nonetheless,

> **Culturally responsive practice**: Strategies that emphasize teachers' cultural knowledge and self-awareness, a commitment to supports that are relevant to their students' cultures and identities, and a focus on decision making to enhance culturally equitable outcomes.

cultural responsiveness cannot be taken for granted as a core component of PBS, and there are critical features of culturally responsive practice we must consider as we craft our classroom management and behavior support practices.

A Culturally Active Approach

As you learned in Chapter 1, School-Wide Positive Behavioral Interventions and Supports (SWPBIS) is an application of PBS that focuses on the entire school (Horner & Sugai, 2015). Earlier conceptualizations of SWPBIS were considered to be 'culturally neutral' in that the model was designed with enough flexibility to be implemented in any school and with any population of students, regardless of their cultural backgrounds (Bal, 2018). However, more recently, SWPBIS implementers have recognized that cultural considerations must be actively incorporated into each aspect of SWPBIS implementation (Leverson et al., 2016). A core element of SWPBIS involves schools developing a 'shared vision of common values, beliefs, and behavior' (Leverson, p. 2). This can only be accomplished when implementers actively seek input from students and their families on what this shared vision should be. One component of Tier 1 SWPBIS involves schools selecting a common set of behavioral expectations for students to follow. As we have learned, culture plays an integral role in determining what behaviors are valued by a particular community. For the shared vision of SWPBIS to be truly inclusive, voices of students, parents, and the community must be actively incorporated into the selection of school-wide expectations. If these voices are ignored, SWPBIS efforts may be rejected.

A culturally active approach to PBS means teachers continually assess how they are taking culture into account in their behavior support efforts. For instance, a key aspect of classroom-level PBS involves teachers creating incentive systems to encourage expected behaviors in the classroom (see Chapter 6). Rather than teachers independently selecting classroom expectations based only on their own values, students should be given the opportunity to provide input on the selection of these expectations. This will help ensure classroom expectations have a good fit with students' cultural values and may increase the likelihood of compliance with expectations that are culturally relevant and consensus based.

In the context of SWPBIS, the School-Wide PBIS Culturally Responsive Tiered

School-Wide PBIS Culturally Responsive Tiered Fidelity Inventory (CR-TFI): A tool to address the fidelity of SWPBIS implementation that includes cultural considerations

Fidelity Inventory (CR-TFI; Algozzine et al., 2014) was designed to assess the fidelity of SWPBIS implementation with cultural considerations in mind. It includes items to assess whether membership of the SWPBIS school team mirrors the composition of the community; student and family voices are incorporated into the development of behavioral expectations; classroom practices are inclusive of students from all racial, cultural, ethnic, linguistic, and ability backgrounds; and outcome data are disaggregated by race, ethnicity, and disability status, to ensure that diverse students are benefitting equally from SWPBIS and not disproportionately subject to punitive discipline practices. Even if your school is not implementing SWPBIS, it is important to consider these key aspects of cultural responsiveness in your approach to classroom management and teaching in general.

High Expectations for All Students

Disproportionately poor educational outcomes for students from diverse racial, ethnic, linguistic, and ability backgrounds is a longstanding and well-documented problem (Gilmour et al., 2019; Lee, 2002; Noguera, 2008). For example, Gilmour et al. found that students with disabilities performed, on average, three years below their peers without disabilities in reading. Similarly, Lee noted pervasive achievement gaps between White students and African American and Latinx students in reading and math in a national sample spanning nearly two decades. The reasons for these documented disparities in educational outcomes are multifaceted and complex. The interplay between poverty and socioeconomic status, early learning experiences, school segregation, unequal school funding, lack of qualified teachers, and widespread use of ineffective teaching practices likely contributes to the achievement gap (Snider, 2006).

Despite the pervasive nature of the problem, evidence-based educational and behavioral interventions, applied with fidelity, can overcome these factors and produce superior educational results for students from diverse racial, ethnic, linguistic, and ability groups (e.g., McIntosh et al., 2018; Stockard et al., 2018; Therrien, 2004). As a teacher, you have limited power to change the broad, complex societal factors that contribute to poor educational outcomes for your students. You do, however, have the ability to adopt empirically supported interventions, including those under the rubric of PBS, that produce measurably superior outcomes for all students. Critical to the successful application of PBS is the expectation that all students can, and will, benefit from your evidence-based behavior support efforts.

Data-Based Decision Making for Equitable Outcomes

As we consider strategies for reducing disparities in punitive school discipline, it is critical we adopt a data-based approach. That is, we actively use data to evaluate whether PBS outcomes are culturally equitable, and where inequities exist, we rely on data to inform our efforts to reduce them. One way to accomplish this is by disaggregating discipline data by race, ethnicity, and disability status, to determine whether diverse groups of students are at greater risk for disciplinary outcomes.

Risk index: The percentage of members of a group experiencing a particular outcome.

Risk ratio: The likelihood of an outcome in one group relative to another group, calculated by dividing the risk index of a target group by the risk index of a comparison group.

McIntosh et al. (2014) offer a straightforward way to examine disproportionality by calculating *risk index* and *risk ratio*. The risk index is the percentage of members of a group experiencing a particular outcome. The risk index can be calculated for any disciplinary outcome for which data are available, including suspension, office discipline referrals, or classroom-level disciplinary actions, such as teacher reprimands. For example, if there are 58 Latinx students enrolled in a school, and 27 have received a suspension, 46.55% of Latinx students received a suspension, a risk index of 0.47. Conversely, if there are 98 White students enrolled in a school, and 27 have received a suspension, 27.55% of White students received a suspension, a risk index of 0.28. Figure 2.1 shows the risk index formula and hypothetical risk index data for various cultural groups and White students in a school's population. The risk index for students with disabilities is calculated separately since there is an overlap between students' disability status and their racial or ethnic group.

Risk ratio is the likelihood of an outcome in one group relative to another group. Risk ratio is one way of expressing a group of students' risk for a particular outcome, in this case, suspension. Risk ratio is calculated by dividing the risk index of the target group by the risk index of the comparison group. If White students are the predominant group in the school, then we can use White students as the comparison group. Alternatively, we can use the entire school's population as a comparison group, which will permit us to examine the risk ratio of a target group relative to the entire school population. If we are interested in evaluating whether students with disabilities are at greater risk for disciplinary outcomes, we can use students without disabilities as the comparison group when calculating their risk ratio.

	# Students Enrolled	# Students Suspended	% Students within Group Suspended	Risk Index
Native	4	1	25.00%	0.25
Asian	27	5	18.52%	0.19
African American	74	44	59.46%	0.59
Latinx	58	27	46.55%	0.47
Pacific	7	2	28.57%	0.29
White	98	27	27.55%	0.28
Unknown	1	0	0.00%	0.00
Not Listed	2	0	0.00%	0.00
TOTAL	271	106	39.11%	0.39
w/ Disabilities	73	42	57.53%	0.58
w/out Disabilities	198	64	32.32%	0.32

$$\frac{\text{Number of Students Receiving Suspension}}{\text{Total Number of Students in the Group}} = \text{Risk Index}$$

$$\frac{\text{Number of Latinx Students Receiving Suspension}}{\text{Total Number of Latinx Students}} = \frac{27}{58} = .47$$

$$\frac{\text{Number of White Students Receiving Suspension}}{\text{Total Number of White Students}} = \frac{27}{98} = .28$$

Figure 2.1 Calculating disciplinary outcomes using a risk index. Adapted from McIntosh, K., Barnes, A., Eliason, B., & Morris, K. (2014). Using discipline data within SWPBIS to identify and address disproportionality: A guide for school teams. OSEP Technical Assistance Center on Positive Behavioral Interventions and Supports. www.pbis.org.

For example, if the risk index of suspension for Latinx students is 0.47 and the risk index of suspension for White students is 0.28, we divide 0.28 by 0.47 to yield a risk ratio of 1.69 for Latinx students. Similarly, if the risk index of suspension for students with disabilities is 0.58 and the risk index of suspension for students without disabilities is 0.32, we divide 0.58 by 0.32 to yield a risk ratio of 1.78 for students with disabilities. Risk ratios of greater than one indicate a higher risk of suspension in both groups of students relative to their comparison groups. In the current examples, Latinx students are 1.69 times more likely to be suspended than White students, and students with disabilities are 1.78 times more likely to be suspended compared with students without disabilities. Examining the risk ratio data in Figure 2.2, we see varying risk for suspension across the groups, with African American, Latinx, and Pacific students at greater risk for suspension relative to White students, and students with disabilities at greater risk for suspension relative to students without disabilities.

There are two possible reasons why students in these groups are at greater risk for suspension: 1) students in the target groups display more challenging

	Native	Asian	African American	Latinx	Pacific	White	Unknown	Not Listed	w/ Disabilities	w/out Disabilities	Total
# Enrolled	4	27	74	58	7	98	1	2	73	198	271
# Suspended	1	5	44	27	2	27	0	0	42	64	106
Risk Index	0.25	0.19	0.59	0.47	0.29	0.28	0.00	0.00	0.58	0.32	0.39
Risk Ratio Compared w/ White	0.91	0.67	2.16	1.69	1.04	1.00	0.00	0.00	N/A	N/A	N/A
Risk Ratio Compared w/ All	0.64	0.47	1.52	1.19	0.73	0.70	0.00	0.00	1.47	0.83	N/A
Risk Ratio Compared w/ out Disabilities	N/A	N/A	N/A	N/A	N/A	N/A	N/A	N/A	N/A	1.78	N/A

$$\frac{\text{Risk Index of the Target Group}}{\text{Risk Index of the Comparison Group}} = \text{Risk Ratio}$$

$$\frac{\text{Risk Index of Latinx Students}}{\text{Risk Index of White Students}} = \frac{.47}{.28} = 1.69$$

$$\frac{\text{Risk Index of Students with Disabilities}}{\text{Risk Index of Students without Disabilities}} = \frac{.58}{.32} = 1.78$$

Figure 2.2 Calculating disciplinary outcomes to determine the risk ratio. Adapted from McIntosh, K., Barnes, A., Eliason, B., & Morris, K. (2014). Using discipline data within SWPBIS to identify and address disproportionality: A guide for school teams. OSEP Technical Assistance Center on Positive Behavioral Interventions and Supports. www.pbis.org.

behaviors, and thus they are disciplined more frequently compared with students in the comparison groups; and/or 2) students in the target groups are more likely to be suspended when they display the same challenging behaviors as students in the comparison groups. It is important to note, however, that when diverse students in a school have higher risk ratios for punitive discipline, we cannot assume it is because they are displaying more challenging behaviors than students in the comparison groups. In fact, research has shown that Black students are more likely than White students to be suspended regardless of their behavior (Morgan et al., 2019). Nonetheless, both scenarios are problematic as they highlight the need for targeted strategies to prevent and reduce challenging behaviors in the groups, and to ensure that students in the groups are not disproportionately subjected to punitive discipline practices like suspension.

Once you or the school team have established that diverse students are at greater risk for disciplinary outcomes compared with White students, students without disabilities, or the entire school population, the following action steps may be applied to reduce disproportionality (see also McIntosh et al.):

1. *Establish goals based on data.* Based on the metrics you calculated to examine disproportionality, select goals to reduce disproportionality in targeted cultural, linguistic, and ability groups. For example, if African American, Latinx, and Pacific students, and students with disabilities, are at greater risk for suspension, the school team might set a goal to reduce suspensions in these populations to a specific number that will result in lower, or at least proportional, risk of suspension relative to White students and students without disabilities.

2. *Analyze possible reasons for disproportionality.* There are myriad reasons why students from a targeted group could disproportionately experience punitive discipline practices. The next step in the process is to identify these possible reasons so we can formulate a plan to address them. For example, if teachers are not using empirically supported instructional practices that allow students from diverse groups to fully participate in lessons, this could produce a higher rate of off-task and other challenging behaviors, which results in more punitive disciplinary consequences for the students. Similarly, if teachers are over-reliant on punitive discipline practices (e.g., reprimand) to the exclusion of positive discipline practices (e.g., redirection and praise) with one or more groups, this can also result in disproportionality. If a school is implementing SWPBIS, failure to adhere to all components with fidelity, or failure to incorporate a culturally active approach (Algozzine et al., 2014), could also increase the exposure of one or more groups to punitive discipline practices. In many cases, disaggregating

data by setting, classroom teacher, grade level, special versus regular education, or subject area will permit a closer examination of whether any of these factors are associated with higher levels of punitive discipline, which sets the occasion for targeted efforts toward reducing disproportionality.

3. *Use evidence-based practice to reduce disproportionality.* As we have discussed, the reasons for poor educational and behavioral outcomes for diverse students are complex and entrenched in a variety of factors, such as students' poverty and socioeconomic status, their early learning experiences, school segregation, unequal school funding, lack of qualified teachers, and widespread use of ineffective teaching practices. Consequently, 'quick fixes' that fail to address these complex factors are unlikely to yield substantive changes that produce robust outcomes (Singal, 2021). For instance, schools may hold workshops and trainings to raise teachers' awareness about systemic racism and conscious and unconscious forms of bias and discrimination. While these efforts may be one important component of a comprehensive approach, if implemented in isolation, they are unlikely to produce meaningful changes given the scope and complex nature of the problem.

In Chapter 1, we discussed the importance of evidence-based practice as a decision-making process to improve educational and behavioral outcomes for students (Slocum et al., 2014). The key to evidence-based practice is using the best available research evidence to guide our educational and behavioral change strategies. There are a variety of empirically supported approaches to change teacher behavior toward reducing disproportionality in school discipline. For example, *behavioral skills training* (BST) has strong empirical support in helping teachers learn a variety of instructional strategies (Kirkpatrick et al., 2019). BST is a strategy to teach skills comprised of instructions, modeling of the skills, opportunities for practice, and performance-based feedback (Sarokoff & Sturmey, 2004). If teachers of diverse students are over-reliant on reprimands in the classroom and use low rates of student praise, we could devise a plan to use BST to increase their use of behavior-specific praise with their students (Pisacreta et al., 2011). Alternatively, if low fidelity implementation of SWPBIS is leading to overuse of punitive discipline practices in the school, we can use BST to train school staff in implementing all aspects of SWPBIS with fidelity or revisit the SWPBIS plan to incorporate more diverse voices into the implementation process.

4. *Use data to evaluate efforts to reduce disproportionality.* After we implement a plan to address disproportionality in punitive discipline, it is critical that we revisit the data to see if our efforts are working. This involves reviewing the data to see whether we have achieved our goals

to reduce the use of punitive discipline practices with diverse groups. Any improvements may be visible in week-by-week, month-by-month, or year-by-year comparisons of data. In addition to examining the use of punitive discipline practices, we should also evaluate whether school staff are employing appropriate alternatives, such as behavior-specific praise, teaching rules and expectations to students, and using classroom-level reward systems (See Chapter 6).

> **Behavioral skills training (BST)**: A strategy to teach skills comprised of instructions, modeling of the skills, opportunities for practice, and performance-based feedback.

Summary

Culture describes the socially learned behaviors, values, preferences, and knowledge specific to a group of people. Cultural diversity includes differences in sexual preference, sexual identity, race and ethnicity, language, political views, religious or atheistic beliefs, and disability. Cultural self-awareness involves understanding your own cultural perspectives and how this affects your interactions with others, including your students. Reflecting on your culture, your students' cultures, and how you can learn more about their cultures can help you become a more culturally responsive classroom manager. Culturally responsive practice emphasizes teachers' cultural knowledge and self-awareness, a commitment to supports that are relevant to their students' cultures and identities, and a focus on data-based decision making to enhance culturally equitable outcomes. A culturally active approach to PBS emphasizes incorporating student, family, and community voices into PBS interventions, and high expectations for all students. Research consistently shows that students from minority groups are disproportionately subjected to punitive discipline practices, and these practices contribute to negative academic outcomes. Calculating the risk index and the risk ratio allows us to evaluate for disproportionality in school discipline at the school-wide or classroom level. We can use these data to inform our evidence-based efforts to reduce disproportionality in punitive school discipline.

Key Terms

Behavioral skills training (BST) – a strategy to teach skills comprised of instructions, modeling of the skills, opportunities for practice, and performance-based feedback.

Culture – The socially learned behaviors, values, preferences, and knowledge specific to a group of people.

Culturally responsive practice – Strategies that emphasize teachers' cultural knowledge and self-awareness, a commitment to supports that are relevant to their students' cultures and identities, and a focus on decision making to enhance culturally equitable outcomes.

Cultural self-awareness – Understanding your own cultural perspectives, others' cultural perspectives, and how these affect your interactions.

Risk index - The percentage of members of a group experiencing a particular outcome.

Risk ratio – The likelihood of an outcome in one group relative to another group, calculated by dividing the risk index of a target group by the risk index of a comparison group.

School-wide PBIS culturally responsive tiered fidelity inventory (CR-TFI) – A tool to address the fidelity of SWPBIS implementation that includes cultural considerations.

Additional Resources

To learn more about culturally responsive PBS, visit the following websites:

Culturally Responsive PBIS Practice Guide: https://www.pbis.org/resource/pbis-cultural-responsiveness-field-guide-resources-for-trainers-and-coaches

Florida Positive Behavioral Interventions and Support Project, Culturally Responsive PBIS: https://flpbis.cbcs.usf.edu/foundations/CR-PBIS.html

Using Discipline Data within SWPBIS to Identify and Address Disproportionality: A Guide for School Teams: https://www.pbis.org/resource/using-discipline-data-within-swpbis-to-identify-and-address-disproportionality-a-guide-for-school-teams

CHAPTER 3

Myths and Facts about Effective Classroom Management

Chapter Objectives

- Understand the Creative Teacher Myth and how to be a critical consumer of classroom management strategies.

- Describe the Bad Student Myth and the role of alterable variables in positive behavior support.

- Explain the Rewards Myth and why rewards are critical to successful classroom management.

- Understand the Punishment Myth and the reasons why punishment should be avoided as a classroom management technique.

- Identify the 'Let's Talk it Out' Myth and how counseling students can worsen their challenging behavior.

DOI: 10.4324/9781003237228-3

In this chapter you will learn about five myths of effective classroom management: the Creative Teacher Myth; the Bad Student Myth; the Rewards Myth; the Punishment Myth; and the 'Let's Talk it Out' Myth. We will explore facts about effective classroom management and how these play a key role in your success as a classroom teacher.

The Creative Teacher Myth

Myth: Creativity is the key to successful classroom management.

Fact: Effective classroom management is not determined by creativity, but by how skillfully the teacher applies systematic, data-based management strategies in the classroom.

Consider this unfortunate scenario. You fall from a ladder and hurt your ankle. It is painful and difficult to walk. Suspecting a broken bone, you visit the emergency room. The doctor examines your ankle and without taking an X-ray prescribes a surprising treatment. 'I've never tried this before. I saw on Pinterest if you rub this cream on your skin it can heal broken bones. It has turmeric in it. It might help with your ankle. Let's try it.' You ask what the cream has to do with healing fractures. 'I'm not sure, but turmeric has natural healing powers.' Skeptical, you ask whether there is any research to show the cream heals fractures. 'I'm not sure, but there's a ton of research on turmeric.' Still skeptical, you seek a second opinion from a different doctor. This doctor X-rays your ankle, diagnoses a fracture, and prescribes a cast. You leave the ER in disbelief, wondering how the first doctor could practice medicine in such an unsystematic way.

Medicine has relied on scientific decision making for many decades, so it is hard to imagine being treated this way by a physician in current times. But many teachers adopt a similar approach to classroom management. When confronted with student behavior problems, they utilize creative, yet unproven strategies to fix them. Educators who use unproven classroom management strategies fail to realize that while virtually any strategy *could* work, those that are based on data and sound research are much more likely to work than those produced by intuition, instinct, creativity, or fad. The field of medicine has been guided by scientifically based practice for many decades. In contrast, the profession of teaching has yet to fully embrace research-based instructional and classroom management practices (Knight et al., 2019).

Teachers cannot be faulted for poor classroom management. In one survey, more than 40% reported that problem behaviors interfered with their teaching (National Center for Education Statistics, 2000), and student misbehavior is consistently associated with higher levels of teacher stress and burnout (Brunsting et al., 2014; Clunies-Ross et al., 2008; O'Brennan et al., 2017; Kokkinos, 2007). Despite the problems associated with challenging behaviors, many teachers report feeling underprepared to manage their classrooms (Mitchell & Arnold, 2004). Students with disabilities, at greater risk of challenging behaviors, are more likely to be included in general education classrooms (Gilmour, 2018). Nonetheless, general education teachers report less training in classroom management techniques compared with special education teachers (Fowler et al., 2017).

In a national survey of teaching preparation programs, Pomerance and Walsh (2020) found that only 14% required candidates to demonstrate proficiency in five evidence-based classroom management strategies. Similarly, in 2009, Arne Duncan, former US Secretary of Education, criticized teacher preparation programs for failing to provide teachers with 'hands-on practical … training about managing the classroom' and strategies on 'how to use data to differentiate and improve instruction and boost student learning.' His criticisms echo concerns expressed by educators about widespread myths of teaching, for example, that good teachers are simply born that way (Snider, 2006) or that structured curricula and learning objectives impede student learning (Heward, 2003). Sadly, these longstanding myths not only inhibit teachers' effectiveness as classroom managers, but they also contribute to marginal test scores, academic failure, drop-out, and other poor outcomes among our students, particularly those who are considered 'hard to teach.'

Fortunately, the fact that you, a current or future teacher, are reading this book attests to your willingness to adopt a more effective approach to classroom management. A rich literature of effective strategies from the field of PBS exists to help you. SWPBIS, a systematic approach to school discipline and classroom management, has been empirically tested in thousands of schools across the United States (Chapter 1; Horner & Sugai, 2015). The success of SWPBIS highlights the importance of systematic, data-based approaches to effective behavior management.

The first step to becoming an effective classroom manager is to be a critical consumer of classroom management approaches. The following questions can guide you when presented with a potential classroom management strategy (see also Heward, 2003).

- ❏ Does the strategy offer an easy fix or magic bullet to solve the problem? If yes, be skeptical.
- ❏ Is the strategy supported by research published in peer-reviewed journals?

❏ Has the strategy been empirically tested in real classrooms with teachers implementing it?

❏ Does the strategy employ data to evaluate student outcomes? How?

The Bad Student Myth

Myth: Some students are just bad and there isn't anything the teacher can do about it.

Fact: Teachers can improve virtually all students' behavior and learning.

Alterable variables: Things the teacher can change to produce improvements in students' learning and behaviors. These include the pace of teaching, responses to problem behaviors, and choice of materials.

Non-alterable variables: Things that affect students' learning and behaviors that are beyond the teacher's control. Examples are disabilities, genes, and poverty.

I teach a behavior management course to beginning teachers. At the beginning of each semester, I pose the following question to the class: Why do students misbehave? Their answers usually fall into two categories. The first is comprised of responses such as, 'Because class is boring,' or 'Their behavior gets the teacher's attention,' or 'The work is too difficult.' The second consists of answers like, 'A disability,' or 'Bad genes,' or 'Poverty.' What is the difference between them? The first category is comprised of responses that refer to *alterable variables*, or things that the teacher can control to alter student learning and behavior (Bloom, 1980; Heward, 2003). For example, the teacher can change her pace of teaching, her responses to problem behaviors, or provide a choice of materials to make class less boring and less likely to trigger student misbehavior. The second refers to *non-alterable variables* or things that are beyond the teacher's control. For instance, the student's disability or genes are not something the teacher can change. Other examples are found in Figure 3.1.

I conduct this activity to draw attention to the Bad Student Myth, that is, due to a variety of reasons – disability, intelligence, genes, poverty, parents, and so on – the student will engage in challenging behaviors and there is little the teacher can do about it. While it is true that these factors influence students' behaviors, they do not necessarily overshadow the effects of good teaching and

Alterable Variables	Non-Alterable Variables
Pace of instruction	Student's disability
Choices in the classroom	Student's community (poverty, crime)
Responses to student problem behaviors	Student's parents
Use of rewards, praise	Student's genes
Activity Schedules	Student's "personality"
Curriculum materials	School administrators
Opportunities for Active Student Responding	Past teachers who didn't do their job

Figure 3.1 Examples of alterable and non-alterable variables.

classroom management. Furthermore, because the teacher's role is to provide good instruction, it is much more productive to focus on the things that you can control – that is, your teaching – than to blame students' challenging behaviors on things beyond your influence.

A common example of the Bad Student Myth occurs when we attribute a student's challenging behaviors to his disability. For example, when a student with autism engages in problem behaviors such as tantrums, I've heard the following explanation: 'He does that because he has autism.' While it is true that students with autism are more prone to engage in certain problem behaviors, these behaviors are often triggered by events in the classroom (e.g., an unstructured schedule) or maintained by specific consequences (e.g., escape from a non-preferred activity). A more useful strategy is to change the classroom environment in ways that will make it unnecessary for the student to engage in such challenging behaviors.

A case study on the application of PBS with Tom, a non-verbal two-year-old with suspected autism who engaged in tantrums (Dunlap & Fox, 1999), illustrates the value of changing alterable variables. Tom's team implemented a multicomponent intervention that included changing his environment to increase predictability, developing consistent expectations across care providers, providing a visual activity schedule, and teaching him to make choices. Figure 3.2 shows how the multicomponent intervention substantially reduced Tom's tantrums across home and childcare settings compared with the baseline. While every child's needs are different, many can be helped with similar multicomponent strategies.

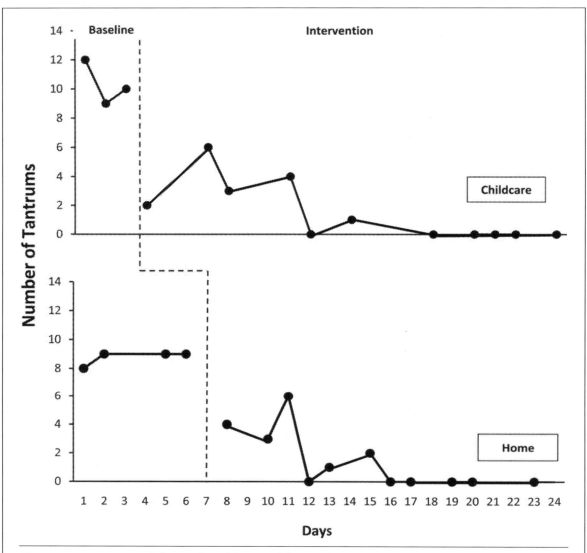

Figure 3.2 How modifying alterable variables with PBS can reduce challenging behaviors. From Dunlap G. & Fox, L. (1999). A demonstration of positive behavioral support for young children with autism. *Journal of Positive Behavior Interventions*, 1, 77–87.

ACTIVITY

Consider a student you know who exhibits challenging behaviors or think of a hypothetical student who exhibits challenging behaviors. What are some ways you could lessen the child's challenging behaviors by changing the classroom environment? As you think about your answer, consider the alterable variables found on the left side of Figure 3.1.

_____

_____

_____

_____

_____

_____

_____

_____

_____

_____

_____

_____

_____

_____

_____

_____

_____

_____

The Rewards Myth

Myth: Rewards and praise undermine students' intrinsic motivation.
Fact: Rewards and praise are both beneficial and necessary to effective classroom management.

Another widespread myth in education involves teachers' use of rewards and praise. It is argued that rewards and praise undermine intrinsic motivation, foster dependence, and ultimately make students less likely to perform the behaviors that teachers are trying to teach. The best-known proponent of this view is the lecturer and author Alfie Kohn (1999), whose anti-reward sentiments have been reflected in classroom management books and texts on student motivation. We will examine how two primary criticisms of rewards and praise are unfounded. These criticisms are that rewards and praise are (a) coercive and (b) don't work in improving students' classroom performance. In contrast, we will explore reasons that rewards and praise are critical to effective classroom management.

Rewards and Praise Are Coercive?

A central tenant of the anti-rewards argument is that the use of rewards, praise, grades, or any attempt to change students' behaviors through consequences is tantamount to coercion because we are controlling them (Kohn). Accordingly, rewarding a student is just as bad as punishing him because we are withholding something favorable if he does not perform in a prescribed manner. Instead, it is argued, students should be provided with engaging materials, choices, and encouragement to 'discover' the correct answers in an environment free of contingencies for performance.

This perspective holds a degree of logic. In an ideal world, students should want to learn for the sake of learning without the need for incentives. Unfortunately, choices, encouragement, and discovery learning are insufficient classroom management tools for a couple of important reasons. First, consequences such as rewards (or, technically, reinforcement) and punishment are principles of human behavior that operate in the classroom irrespective of the teacher's management techniques (see Chapter 6) (Cooper et al., 2020; Maag, 2001). Students will always do things to produce consequences, whether it's attention from a teacher, approval from a parent, or recognition from their peers. Rewards in the broader sense don't go away because teachers stop using reward systems – like gravity, they are just there. Teachers who fail to use rewards and praise systematically risk inadvertently reinforcing students' challenging behaviors. For example, a preschool student who needs help with her scissors discovers that loudly screaming is an effective way to get the teacher's attention. A more practical and productive approach is to capitalize on rewards and praise to prevent challenging behaviors. In this case, we could teach the student an alternative, appropriate way to get the teacher's attention (e.g., by raising her hand) and reward her for performing this alternative response. We will learn specific strategies for using praise and rewards to teach alternative behaviors in the following chapters.

Second, rewards and punishment are not equal outcomes in any sense. Virtually anyone would choose to be rewarded for doing something good than to be punished for doing something bad. There is overwhelming evidence to suggest that reward systems enhance student motivation and engagement when used appropriately; in a meta-analysis of 101 studies, Cameron and Pierce (1994) found that, overall, praise increased students' intrinsic motivation to engage in tasks. Praise only had a negative effect on intrinsic motivation when it was applied without regard to the quality of students' performance. In contrast, punishment-based discipline systems, all too common in schools, result in higher rates of problem behaviors and lower academic achievement (Horner et al., 2009; Sugai & Horner, 2002). In the absence of rewards and praise, students may discover what to do, but in many cases, they may discover how to do something bad.

Rewards and Praise Don't Work?

Another argument against using rewards and praise is that they don't work. It is argued that rewards and praise may temporarily increase student compliance, but they also foster dependence and, when withdrawn, students lose their desire to perform (Kohn, 1999). Again, this argument possesses some logic – we do not want students to depend on feedback each time they perform a response. Still, one wonders what highly paid professional athletes, specialist physicians, and CEOs – all of whom are well rewarded for their work – think about the idea of rewards *undermining* their performance?

The question is not whether rewards work – they certainly do; however, research shows that rewards are effective only if they are applied according to specific guidelines. For instance, Cameron

> **Thinning the schedule of reinforcement**: The process of gradually decreasing how frequently you deliver reinforcement (e.g., praise, rewards) to a student. This can be accomplished by increasing the number of responses required to earn reinforcement, or by increasing the amount of time with appropriate behavior that must pass before the student earns reinforcement.

and Pierce (1994) found that praise and feedback increased students' intrinsic motivation only when applied after students met a specific standard of performance. So, it is important for teachers to recognize and reward both the *quality* and *accuracy* of students' responses. The concept of *thinning the schedule of reinforcement* is also critical to using rewards and praise effectively (Cooper et al., 2020). When initially teaching a skill, you should apply praise and feedback more frequently, perhaps after every response or every other response, on average. Then, you should gradually thin the schedule of reinforcement, so that you give praise and feedback after every third response, every fifth response, every tenth response, and so forth. In this manner, students lose their 'dependency' on rewards and require feedback only occasionally to maintain their skills. How you quickly thin the schedule of reinforcement depends on the student and the skill.

In Chapter 2, we learned that diverse students are at greater for punitive discipline practices, including suspension, compared with White students (e.g., Morgan et al., 2019). Thus, one important component of culturally responsive PBS is implementing strategies to reduce disparities in punitive school discipline by race, ethnicity, and ability status. To reduce schools' overreliance on these practices, we must use effective, alternative strategies that are not punishment-based. Rewards, praise, and other forms of positive reinforcement are the best alternatives to punishment-based discipline practices for reducing disparities in school discipline.

Behavior-specific praise (BSP) is when a teacher provides praise following a behavior by describing the behavior in specific terms (e.g., 'I like the way you *raised your hand*') (see Chapter 6). BSP can be contrasted with general praise that does not describe the behavior that resulted in praise (e.g., 'Nice working'), or otherwise does not describe any malleable behavior within the student's control (e.g., 'You are so smart!'). Royer et al. (2019) conducted a systematic review on the effects of BSP on student behaviors in the classroom, including inappropriate behavior, disruptive behavior, off-task behavior, and on-task behavior. They identified six published studies that met contemporary standards for high-quality research. All six studies showed that BSP demonstrated positive outcomes on these variables, in that BSP reduced inappropriate, disruptive, and off-task behaviors, and increased on-task behavior. Five of the studies demonstrated large treatment effects on the targeted outcomes. Royer et al.'s results show how BSP can be an effective, reinforcement-based approach for improving prosocial behavior in the classroom.

Behavior-specific praise (BSP): Providing praise following a behavior by describing the behavior in specific terms.

ACTIVITY

Imagine that you are a teacher who is beginning a new reward system with a group of your students. After sending a note home to inform parents about the new system, you receive a phone call from one parent who expresses concerns about the use of rewards with his daughter. Specifically, he is worried that she will no longer be motivated to do her work unless someone offers her treats, gold stars, and other classroom incentives. How would you respond to his concerns and convince him that a reward system is appropriate and useful for his child?

_____

_____

_____

_____

_____

_____

_____

_____

_____

_____

_____

_____

_____

_____

_____

_____

_____

The Punishment Myth

Myth: Students with challenging behaviors need strict discipline, including punishment.

Fact: Punishment can worsen challenging behaviors.

The next myth of classroom management is that students who display problem behaviors need stern discipline and punishment. It is hard to say how this myth originated – the concept of punishment is deeply embedded in both our culture generally and in the field of education specifically. Maag (2001) offers several reasons why teachers rely heavily on reprimands, detentions, suspensions, and expulsions to control students' behaviors. First, these procedures tend to produce immediate, if temporary, cessations in problem responses. For instance, the student who misbehaves and is sent to detention is no longer irritating to the teacher (or other students). Second, punishment – or the threat of punishment -- is effective for many students who display low rates of problem behaviors and comprise the majority of the school's population. Third, educators have largely ignored the data supporting the use of positive techniques (e.g., Cameron & Pierce, 1994), perhaps as a function of myths about rewards perpetuated by Kohn (1999) and others.

Punishment should be used sparingly for two important reasons. First, because punishment tends to produce immediate cessation of students' problem behaviors, teachers may be tempted to over-rely on punishment techniques in the classroom (Shook, 2012). When overused, punishment leads to undesirable side effects, for example, students will avoid the people and environments where punishment occurs or will engage in aggressive or disruptive responses toward the person administering punishment (Lee & Axelrod, 2005). Second, techniques such as detention and time-out that are intended to reduce problem behaviors often result in the opposite effect (Maag, 2001). Consider the student who dislikes math, makes abusive comments to his classmates during class, and is sent by the teacher to in-school detention. Sending the student to detention may actually reinforce inappropriate comments by allowing the student to escape from math class. Too often, punishment procedures are applied in this fashion without regard to the function of problem behaviors (see Chapter 6). In contrast, because positive techniques lack the side effects associated with punishment, they should always be the teacher's first choice when considering behavior management strategies. We will explore considerations for using positive behavior support techniques throughout the remainder of the book.

The 'Let's Talk It Out' Myth

Myth: Talking with students resolves their problem behaviors.

Fact: As a reactive strategy, talking with students seldom reduces their challenging behaviors, and can make their behaviors worse.

The final myth of classroom management comes from a commonsense idea about students' challenging behaviors. That is, when students misbehave, if we can just talk with them, understand the reasons for their misbehavior, explain to them why their behavior is wrong, and offer alternatives, they will misbehave less. While 'talking it out' isn't a formal classroom management approach per se, teachers may default to this strategy in the absence of sound training in evidence-based classroom management techniques (Shook, 2012).

We do not want to discourage teachers from building rapport with their students by talking to them. Talking with your students is a great way to get to know them, their interests, and their personalities. However, there are several pitfalls to 'talking it out' as a reactive strategy in response to problem behaviors. First, as we discussed earlier in the chapter, students may perform challenging behaviors to produce a variety of consequences, which include gaining someone's attention. For example, in a second-grade classroom of 30 students, where the teacher is understandably busy and seldom provides individual attention to students, Eva has learned that shouting during seatwork can be a very effective way to get her teacher's attention. That is, when Eva doesn't understand the instructions for an assignment, she shouts, her teacher immediately walks over and asks, 'What's wrong?', clarifies the problem, and provides Eva assistance. However, the teacher's response may encourage Eva to talk out in the future because she has learned this is the best way to get their attention in the busy classroom if she needs assistance.

Teachers also may be tempted to 'talk it out' because they believe if students understand why their behavior is problematic, they will stop doing it. This is unlikely to work for a couple of key reasons. First, due to their ages and/or developmental levels, many students lack the cognitive and reasoning skills to fully understand the nature and consequences of their behavior. Second, even if they do understand why their behavior is wrong, it is still unlikely to change as long as it is reinforced by teacher attention, escape from aversive situations, or other powerful consequences in the classroom setting (Durand & Carr, 1991). Consider adults who engage in one of the most harmful behaviors known to medical science, smoking cigarettes. Virtually all adults in our society understand the deleterious health effects of smoking, yet many continue to do it because of the powerful addictive consequences of nicotine dependence (Mayer et al., 2020). If understanding the consequences of harmful behaviors was sufficient to eliminate them, smoking would cease to be a public health problem, and classroom management would be a far easier task.

So what are the alternatives to 'talking it out' in response to problem behaviors? First, if the teacher is implementing the classroom management systems described in the later chapters of this book, posted classroom rules, classroom-reward systems for students following the rules, strategies for promoting active student response, and individualized behavior support plans where indicated, the need for reactive strategies should be minimized. In cases where teachers must respond to challenging behaviors, they should consider the following tips. If a student misbehaves and you must attend to the behavior because it is disruptive or even dangerous, provide as little attention as necessary to redirect the student. If a behavior is potentially dangerous (e.g., physical fighting, major property destruction), the teacher may need to seek assistance from other school staff or move students away from each other; however, this should also be done in a calm, neutral fashion.

Summary

There are five myths of effective classroom management. The first myth is that creativity is the key to successful classroom management. This myth is false because good classroom managers rely less on creativity and more on empirically supported strategies to foster student success. The second is that some students are just bad and there is little the teacher can do about it. This myth is false because the teacher can improve most students' behaviors by addressing alterable variables. The third myth is that rewards don't work to improve students' performance. This myth is false because research shows that praise and rewards, when applied correctly, do improve students' learning and behavior. The fourth myth is that punishment is necessary for good classroom management. This myth is false because punishment is often overused and can lead to undesirable side effects. Instead, teachers should rely on positive techniques when possible. The final myth is that 'talking it out' with a student reduces their challenging behavior. This myth is false because understanding the consequences of challenging behavior does not necessarily produce behavior change. Alternatively, teachers should rely on proactive behavior management systems, and provide the minimal attention necessary when they must respond to challenging behaviors.

Key Terms

Alterable variables – Things the teacher can change to produce improvements in students' learning and behaviors. These include the pace of teaching, responses to problem behaviors, and choice of materials.

Behavior-specific praise (BSP) – Providing praise following a behavior by describing the behavior in specific terms.

Non-alterable variables – Things that affect students' learning and behaviors that are beyond the teacher's control. Examples are disabilities, genes, and poverty.

Thinning the schedule of reinforcement – The process of gradually decreasing how frequently you deliver reinforcement (e.g., praise, rewards) to a student. This can be accomplished by increasing the number of responses required to earn reinforcement or by increasing the amount of time with appropriate behavior that must pass before the student earns reinforcement.

CHAPTER 4

The Foundation
Classroom Organization

Chapter Objectives

- Describe how consistency and planning are critical to preventing challenging behaviors.

- Identify the guidelines for developing student schedules.

- Recognize the characteristics of the whole class and individual student schedules and considerations for designing each.

- Explain how to effectively organize the physical space of your classroom.

- Describe the qualities of efficient activity transitions.

- Identify strategies for effectively working with teaching assistants.

DOI: 10.4324/9781003237228-4

In this chapter, we will focus on the foundation of effective management, classroom organization. Organizing your classroom requires an initial investment of time and effort; however, it pays off by lessening the amount of time you spend managing students' behaviors. You will learn how organizing schedules, the physical space of your classroom, student groupings, and working effectively with teaching assistants can improve your students' independence and knowledge of the classroom routine.

Student Schedules

Consistency and Planning Are Key

Remember that a critical feature of PBS is arranging the classroom environment to *prevent* challenging behaviors (see Chapter 1). As a rule, students perform fewer challenging behaviors and are more engaged when the classroom schedule is organized, structured, and consistent (Oliver et al., 2011). A consistent schedule familiarizes students with the routine and helps to communicate your expectations for their performance. A consistent schedule means that activities start and stop at the same time each day and occur in a predictable, predetermined sequence to the extent possible.

It is equally important to ensure that all of your instructional time is planned. For example, if students finish an independent seatwork assignment early, is there a specific activity for them to work on for the remainder of the period? Unplanned downtime gives students the opportunity to misbehave. In contrast, creating schedules helps to ensure that all of a student's instructional time is carefully arranged.

Guidelines for Developing Student Schedules

Consider the following guidelines as you develop your students' schedules.

Alternate demanding and preferred activities. Some classroom activities are more demanding than others. For instance, a math lesson is more likely to evoke student frustration than an activity comprised of free time playing games on phones, tablets, or desktop computers. One way to prevent challenging behaviors is to arrange the schedule so that you alternate demanding and preferred activities. This strategy capitalizes on the *Premack principle* (Premack, 1963; Cooper et al., 2020). The strategy, also known as Grandma's rule, is observed at dinner tables when parents reward their children with the opportunity to eat dessert (higher probability behavior) if they first eat a non-preferred food, such as vegetables (lower probability behavior).

In the classroom context, the Premack principle is an application of positive reinforcement, in which the opportunity to engage in a higher probability behavior (e.g., playing games) reinforces a lower probability behavior (e.g., solving algebra equations).

Premack principle: An application of positive reinforcement, in which the opportunity to engage in a higher probability behavior reinforces a lower probability behavior.

In one study, Rattan and Wrightington (2020) incorporated the Premack principle into an individualized activity schedule to increase written work completion of a high school student with autism spectrum disorder. In the baseline condition, the student was asked to complete written work in algebra, science, history, and English. He completed an average of only 14% of his work during baseline. During intervention, his educational team implemented a visual 'First Then' visual activity schedule in which each written academic assignment was followed by the opportunity to engage in a preferred activity. The preferred activities used in the study – reading comic books, playing math games on a tablet computer, and playing board games – were determined through interviews with the student's teacher, paraprofessional, parents, and the student himself. The activity schedule increased his written work completion to an average of 29% to 61% across an eight-week period. During the final three weeks of the intervention, his highest levels of work productivity were observed as the team gave him a choice menu of preferred activities after each assignment.

Similarly, Figure 4.1 shows two schedules. The one on the left consists of demanding activities ordered consecutively. The one on the right is revised so that demanding and preferred activities are alternated.

Break up long activities. Even a preferred activity can become boring if it lasts for too long. Consider breaking up lengthy activities to increase student engagement. For example, if your English period lasts for 45 minutes and you assign a vocabulary activity, you could have students work independently for 20 minutes, exchange papers with a partner to correct their work for 15 minutes, and then review the correct answers as a whole class for ten

Consecutive Demanding Activities	Demanding and Preferred Activities Interspersed
Reading	**Reading**
Social Studies	Computer-time
Math	**Social Studies**
Computer-time	Free-play
Break	**Math**
Free-play	Break
Lunch	Lunch

Figure 4.1 Two student schedules. The left schedule has demanding activities ordered consecutively. The right schedule has demanding and preferred activities interspersed.

minutes. Breaking up activities in this manner adds variety and decreases the likelihood of boredom and problem behaviors.

Choice making: Providing students with an opportunity to make limited and reasonable choices in the context of classroom routines to promote self-determination and prosocial behaviors.

Offer choices. Choice making allows students to access reinforcing items and activities through appropriate behaviors and helps students to become self-determined learners (Wood et al., 2005). There are many ways to incorporate choice into the daily classroom routine. For instance, you can allow students to choose the location of the classroom where they work, the materials they use, the order in which they complete assignments, or the partner they work with. Importantly, you should offer *limited choices* rather than *open-ended choices*. For instance, you should give students a choice of two specific locations in the classroom to work rather than just letting them work anywhere they choose.

ACTIVITY

Mr. Rodriguez teaches middle school science. He is currently working with his students on a unit about the earth's geology, focusing on how volcanoes are formed. He asks students to work in groups of two to conduct a presentation about a famous volcano. He decides to incorporate choices into the project to enhance students' motivation to complete the project. After some reflection, he devises strategies to incorporate choice into the project along the following dimensions:

- *Groupings*: Mr. Rodriguez gives students an opportunity to pick the partner they will work with; he reviews each partnering and makes the final determination as to which students will work together.
- *Locations*: When students work together on the project during class time, he gives them a choice of where they work in the classroom. Students can continue to choose their work location, as long as they work together productively.
- *Assignment features*: From a group of well-known volcanoes, he allows students to pick which volcano they will focus on for their project.
- *Modalities*: As the culminating activity for the project, he asks students to give a presentation to the class using technology. He gives students a choice of which app they will use to present (i.e., Google Slides, PowerPoint, Canva, Prezi) based on their experiences using presentation apps for similar previous projects.

Now, think of an example assignment or unit that you might teach. Describe the basic dimensions of the unit. Then, identify ways you could incorporate choice into the assignment or unit.

Unit or assignment:

_____

_____

_____

_____

_____

Dimensions of choice:

- Groupings:

  _____

  _____

  _____

- Locations:

  _____

  _____

  _____

- Assignment Features:

  _____

  _____

  _____

  _____

- Modalities:

  _____

  _____

  _____

- Others (e.g., materials, rewards, order of tasks):

  _____

  _____

  _____

  _____

Whole class schedules. A whole class schedule defines what the entire class is going to be doing for the school day. Typically, the whole class schedule aligns with the day's instructional periods (e.g., Period 1 – Math, Period 2 – Life Skills, Period 3 – Reading, etc.). Creating a whole class schedule is fairly straightforward; however, there are two important considerations as you develop the schedule. First, the whole class schedule should be prominently posted and clearly readable to students and adults in the classroom. Therefore, the lettering of the schedule should be large enough for everyone to read and it should be placed in a highly visible location (e.g., in the front of the room).

Second, it is helpful if the schedule can be revised to accommodate any changes in the daily routine, such as assemblies, standardized testing, or early dismissals. Writing the schedule on the classroom's dry erase board, as shown in Figure 4.2, enables you to make these revisions to accommodate any changes in the daily routine.

> **Whole class schedule**: A publicly posted schedule that depicts what the entire class is doing throughout the entire school day.

Importantly, at the beginning of the school year, you should introduce the whole class schedule to your students by verbally reviewing the day's planned activities before the first period. As students learn the routine, you can revisit the schedule to remind students about the day's activities along with any anticipated changes. A clear, prominently posted schedule serves as a visual reminder for students about the day's activities and is an integral component of a highly organized classroom.

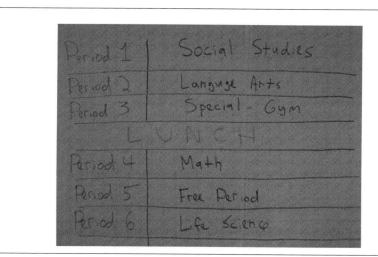

Figure 4.2 Example of a whole class schedule.

Individual student schedule: A personalized written or pictorial schedule that lists the activities a student is supposed to do throughout the school day.

Individual student schedules. Some students need personalized schedules to help them learn the daily routine. Like whole class schedules, *individual student schedules* prevent challenging behaviors by making the classroom routine structured and predictable (Massey & Wheeler, 2000; Spriggs et al., 2007; Zimmerman et al., 2017). Individual student schedules are not unlike the pocket calendars or smartphones that adults use to organize themselves. They can be written and pictorial. Figures 4.3 and 4.4 show examples of written and pictorial student schedules.

Which students need activity schedules? Virtually all students benefit from some type of individualized organizational system. Secondary students can use the same types of calendars and schedules that adults use. Younger students and students with intellectual disabilities may require simplified schedules,

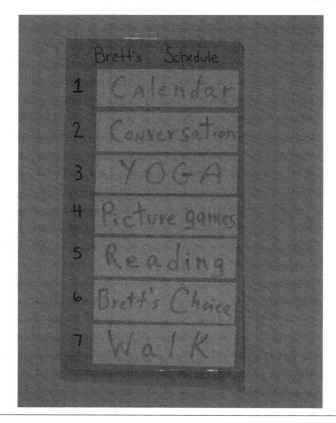

Figure 4.3 Example of a written activity schedule.

Figure 4.4 Example of a pictorial activity schedule.

such as the ones you see in Figures 4.3 and 4.4. If the student can read, the schedule should be written at the students' reading level. If the student cannot read, then a pictorial schedule is the best choice.

There are a few guidelines to consider as you develop individual student schedules. First, when possible, it is important to involve the student in creating the schedule. For secondary students, this could mean allowing them to select the type and order of activities for the day. For younger students or students with intellectual disabilities, this could mean selecting one or two points in the schedule to provide a choice between activities. Remember that it is best to provide a limited choice between two or three activities rather than to provide an open-ended choice.

The schedule should be reviewed in advance to give students a heads up about the order of activities for the day. This could be accomplished by having the student write out the schedule before first period or, if the student is using a pictorial schedule, assisting the student in setting up the day's schedule by putting the picture symbols in the correct sequence. Similarly, you should preview any anticipated changes at the beginning of the day. For instance, if there is a special assembly during third period, homeroom is an excellent opportunity to draw the child's attention to this special event.

For students with access to phones, tablets, or laptops, there are myriad apps available to create individualized schedules. For example, iPhones and Android devices have calendar apps that come pre-installed and/or are freely available, like Google Calendar and Outlook, that can be used to create activity schedules. For students with moderate or significant disabilities, there are specialized apps for creating individualized visual activity schedules, such as

First Then Visual Schedule, which is available in the Apple App Store and the Google Play Store. Douglas and Uphold (2014) evaluated the effects of an electronic picture activity schedule, created with the First Then Visual Schedule, on task completion of five high school students with intellectual disabilities. During baseline, the students were asked to complete a classroom task with minimal assistance from the teacher. Then, during intervention, they were taught to create and use a visual schedule on the iPad or iPod Touch with First Then Visual Schedule to complete the task. For all five students, the use of the electronic visual activity schedule corresponded with a substantial increase in their percentage of correctly completed task steps. Their use of the schedule also generalized to a novel activity and device that was not taught to them.

ACTIVITY

Imagine that it is the beginning of the school year and you are developing whole class and individual activity schedules for your students. Make a hypothetical whole class activity schedule for your classroom incorporating the considerations we have discussed. Then, design an individual activity schedule for a student with or without a disability that is likely to lessen the likelihood of challenging behaviors.

Organized Physical Space

The physical space of your classroom, including desk arrangements, also affects students' success (Rosenfield et al., 1985; Wannarka & Ruhl, 2008). A neat classroom with organized shelves, clearly posted schedules, and recent samples of student work creates an environment for learning. In contrast, a messy or disorganized classroom with unclear physical boundaries communicates lowered expectations to your students. Consider the following guidelines as you organize the physical space of your classroom.

Clearly Defined Instructional Areas

The physical spaces of your classroom should be organized into clearly defined instructional areas. For example, the materials for reading, language arts, social studies, and math lessons should be in separate places within the classroom. Shelves and centers should have clear visual boundaries and cues to reflect their respective purposes. These could include colored tape (e.g., red for reading versus blue for math), picture symbols, and written signs. As with schedules, clearly defined instructional areas establish consistency and help students to learn the classroom routine.

It is also beneficial to create places in the classroom where students can turn in assignments and gather instructional materials. For instance, placing a folder for homework near the classroom door enables students to drop off completed assignments as they enter the classroom. Similarly, creating folders and shelves for students to gather specific lesson materials (e.g., worksheets, workbooks, pencils, markers) helps them to become more independent and frees the teacher from having to distribute materials during transitions and lessons.

Seating Arrangements

Student seating arrangements will vary depending on the nature of your students and the classroom activity. Low achieving students who display challenging behaviors may benefit from sitting closer to the teacher or in the front of the room (Heron & Harris, 2001). In contrast, students who work well independently can be placed farther from the teacher and instructional stimuli.

Desks should be positioned strategically to accommodate specific activities and students. For example, if students are working on a cooperative group activity, desks can be arranged in clusters to facilitate dialogue and sharing of ideas (Heron et al., 2003). The traditional row pattern of desks is best suited for individual student work, while the horseshoe pattern can facilitate discussion during whole class activities (Wannarka & Ruhl, 2008). Do not be afraid to change desk or seating arrangements to facilitate cooperative learning and prosocial behaviors.

Considering 'Traffic' Patterns and Student Distractibility

It is important to think about how traffic patterns in your room will influence students' concentration as they work. For instance, if children frequently transition in and out of your classroom during instructional periods, it is a good idea to position distractible students away from the classroom door. Likewise, if there is an area of your classroom that might draw students' attention from their work (e.g., computer or free play area), it makes sense to position distractible students away from it.

Students with Physical Disabilities

Students with physical disabilities, particularly those with impairments that limit mobility, require special consideration as you arrange your classroom. Students who use wheelchairs or other assistive devices will need ample space to move around the room. The following questions bear consideration:

- ❏ Are entrance ways, the spaces in between desks, and the spaces in front of shelves wide enough for students with limited mobility to navigate?
- ❏ Are instructional materials placed in close proximity so that students do not have to move across the classroom to access them?
- ❏ Are instructional materials placed on shelves so that they are in arms reach?

ACTIVITY

You are rearranging the physical space of your classroom to better accommodate students with and without disabilities. Draw a map of your classroom depicting how instructional areas (e.g., student desks, student seats), your desk, storage, shelves, instructional materials, and so on will be arranged. Consider how you will organize your classroom to maximize students' attention to instruction and ability to move around and access instructional materials in a distraction-free manner.

Efficient Activity Transitions

Orderly activity transitions are critical to good classroom management. It is important that transitions are as brief as possible; they should be just long enough for students to move from one area of the room to another, gather instructional materials, and then begin the lesson. Two to three minutes should be a sufficient interval for an organized transition within your classroom. A clear cue to signal the end of one activity and the beginning of the next is helpful to facilitate brief transitions. Some teachers use visual and auditory devices such as electronic timers as cues for transitions. These cues have an additional benefit of providing feedback to students about how much time they have left to complete an activity.

Transitions will be smoother if your lesson prep has been completed *before* the lesson begins. This means that textbooks, worksheets, and other lesson materials are ready when the activity starts. If you are still prepping as your lesson begins, this will create additional downtime and will provide the opportunity for students to misbehave.

Effectively Working with Teaching Assistants

In Chapter 1, we learned that PBS interventions emphasize *stakeholder participation*. As members of the educational team, teaching assistants are critical stakeholders in your students' academic success and can help you create an organized classroom environment. For example, teaching assistants can assist with lesson prep, provide praise and rewards for students' appropriate behaviors, and help students who need individualized assistance with classroom assignments. The following guidelines will help you to maximize the effectiveness of your teaching assistants.

❏ Make your performance expectations explicit. Teaching assistants will be more helpful if you clearly communicate your expectations for their role. One way to accomplish this is to create a schedule that delineates what you, the teacher, and the teaching assistants will do throughout the day. For instance, as you are finishing one lesson, the teaching assistant(s) can prepare materials for the next. This will facilitate smooth, brief transitions. Or, as you are delivering the lesson to the whole group, the teaching assistant(s) can provide individualized help to specific students who need it. Figure 4.5 shows a sample daily schedule for a self-contained special education classroom, which delineates staff and student assignments throughout the day. Just like

Period	Ms. Munoz - Teacher	Mr. Harris – TA 1	Ms. Lawson – TA 2	Ms. Cicci – TA 3
7:30 – 8:15 – Arrival / Check in	Check homework; review daily schedules	Phillip and Eva	Diante and Sam	Chris, Luiz, and Colin
8:15 – 9:00 - Math	Teach lesson	Phillip and Eva	Diante and Sam	Chris, Luiz, and Colin
9:00 – 9:45 - PE	Prep	Diante and Sam	Chris, Luiz, and Colin	Phillip and Eva
9:45 – 10:30 – Science	Teach lesson	Chris, Luiz, and Colin	Phillip and Eva	Diante and Sam
10:30 – 11:15 - Independent work	Phillip and Eva	Chris, Luiz, and Colin	Lunch	Diante and Sam
11:15 – 12:00 - Lunch	Lunch	Lunch	Chris, Luiz, and Colin	Diante, Sam, Phillip and Eva
12:00 – 12:45 – English	Chris, Luiz, and Colin	Diante and Sam	Phillip and Eva	Lunch
12:45 – 1:30 – Vocational	Prep; support TAs as needed	Diante and Sam	Chris, Luiz, and Colin	Phillip and Eva
1:30 – 2:15 – Social Studies	Teach lesson	Phillip and Eva	Chris, Luiz, and Colin	Diante and Sam
2:15 – 2:30 – Pack up	Review homework and next day schedule	Chris, Luiz, and Colin	Diante and Sam	Phillip and Eva

Figure 4.5 Sample teacher/teaching assistant student staffing schedule.

student activity schedules, teacher and teaching assistant activity schedules should be written and posted or easily available to staff in the classroom.

❑ Provide ongoing feedback. It is important to communicate with your teaching assistants at least once per week about their performance. Weekly scheduled team meetings are a convenient time to discuss staff performance. If you must provide corrective feedback, be sure to identify at least one positive aspect of their performance to praise.

Summary

Classroom organization is critical to preventing challenging behaviors. Organization and planning are key aspects of effective classroom management. Students benefit from both whole class and individual student activity schedules. Whole class schedules should be clearly posted, reviewed with students, and revised as appropriate. Individual student schedules can be written, pictorial, or incorporated into technology, and can be used to promote choice making. Organizing the physical space of your classroom means having clearly defined instructional areas and desk arrangements that promote on-task behaviors and learning. Your classroom should also be arranged to promote the mobility of students with physical disabilities. Effective activity transitions are brief, with a clear signal to cue the beginning and end of activities. Finally, when working with teaching assistants, you should make your expectations for their performance explicit and provide ongoing feedback.

Key Terms

Choice making – Providing students with an opportunity to make limited and reasonable choices in the context of classroom routines to promote self-determination and prosocial behaviors.

Individual student schedule – A personalized written or pictorial schedule that lists the activities a student is supposed to do throughout the school day.

Premack principle – An application of positive reinforcement, in which the opportunity to engage in a higher probability behavior reinforces a lower probability behavior.

Whole class schedule – A publicly posted schedule that depicts what the entire class is doing throughout the entire school day.

CHAPTER 5

Active Student Responding to Prevent Challenging Behaviors

Chapter Objectives

- Define active student responding (ASR).

- Describe how ASR is critical to preventing students' challenging behaviors during instruction.

- Recognize how to use response cards, choral responding, and guided notes to promote high rates of ASR for all students.

- Identify how brisk instructional pacing increases ASR.

- Describe technology-based strategies for increasing ASR.

DOI: 10.4324/9781003237228-5

This chapter will focus on how teachers can promote high rates of active student responding to prevent challenging behaviors and enhance academic success. First, we will define active student responding and discuss how it is essential to good classroom management and instruction. Then, we will explore strategies for promoting active student responding. The strategies are response cards, choral responding, guided notes, and brisk instructional pacing.

What Is Active Student Responding?

Imagine that you are visiting a school to observe a fourth-grade social studies class. The teacher stands at the front of the room while asking questions about the week's lesson topic, China. A few students eagerly attend to the teacher and raise their hands each time he asks a question. Others seem less interested and occasionally raise their hands to offer an answer. About a third of the class looks bored, seldom participates, and several students are talking to their neighbors, laughing, and engaging in other off-task behaviors.

You move to another classroom and notice that students have dry erase boards on their desks. This teacher is delivering a similar lesson, but her students are much more engaged. Each time she asks a question, students quickly write answers on their dry erase boards and raise the boards to reveal their answers. All of the students in this lively classroom are responding, and you see very few off-task behaviors among the group.

Active student responding: When a student emits a detectable response to ongoing instruction, such as saying, writing, or typing an answer.

The difference between the first and second classrooms illustrates the value of active student responding (ASR). According to Heward (1994), 'ASR occurs when a student emits a detectable response to ongoing instruction' (p. 286). Examples of ASR include saying answers to teacher-posed questions, writing answers to math problems, or typing responses on a keyboard. ASR can be contrasted with unobservable or passive student responding. For example, a teacher presents a lesson and students 'think' or 'reflect' on their answers, or they observe other students respond, but they do not themselves perform observable responses.

Some instructional strategies are better at producing high rates of ASR than others. For instance, a teacher who presents math problems and asks students to answer by raising their hands is likely to have low rates of ASR because students can only respond one at a time. In contrast, a teacher who briskly presents math problems and then asks all students to respond by writing answers on dry erase boards will have much higher rates of ASR and participation, overall.

Why is ASR critical to good classroom management and teaching? There are two important reasons. First, the more students are actively responding during instruction, the more likely they are to learn the curriculum, regardless of content (Greenwood et al., 1984). Second, increasing students' rates of ASR decreases their off-task and other challenging behaviors, and increases their academic engagement (Lambert et al., 2006; MacSuga-Gage et al., 2015; Tincani & Crozier, 2007). Simply put, the more students emit active responses, the less opportunity they have to engage in disruptive behaviors. High rates of ASR produce appropriate behaviors that are incompatible with challenging behaviors.

Promoting Active Student Responding

You will learn four strategies for increasing ASR in the classroom: response cards; choral responding; guided notes; and brisk instructional pacing. Importantly, each of these strategies can be used regardless of the subject area or curriculum.

Response Cards

The vignette at the beginning of this chapter illustrates one strategy for promoting ASR, *response cards* (Heward, 1994; Lambert et al., 2006; Tincani & Twyman, 2016). Students either write their answers on their response cards or,

> **Response cards**: Write-on or preprinted cards on which students write or select answers during teacher-directed lessons.

if the cards are preprinted, select the correct answer from an array. Figure 5.1 shows write-on response cards and Figure 5.2 shows preprinted response cards.

Response cards can be made inexpensively. This makes them an attractive option to promote ASR of students who attend schools with limited financial resources, including those that serve diverse students. The most cost-effective way to make write-on response cards is to visit your local home improvement store and purchase a sheet of bathroom board, which is used to line showers and bathtubs. It is often found in the lumber section of the store. Most home improvement stores will cut the boards into 8.5" × 11" pieces for you to create a set of individual response cards for your class. The bathroom board surface is completely erasable with a dry erase marker. This type of response card is shown in Figure 4.1.

Preprinted response cards can be made by laminating sheets of paper, as you see in Figure 5.2. Typically, students use an object, such as a clothespin,

Figure 5.1 Write-on response cards.

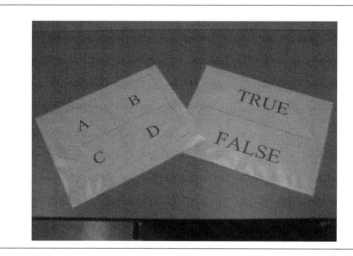

Figure 5.2 Preprinted response cards.

to select the correct answer. Both true/false and multiple-choice responses can be made on preprinted response cards. For instance, Godfrey et al. (2003) conducted a study in which they asked preschool students 'What season?' and the students selected fall, winter, spring, or summer on a preprinted response card. Preprinted response cards are ideal for younger students, or for students who lack sufficient writing proficiency to use write-on response cards.

In Chapter 2, we discussed the importance of instructional methods that allow for the participation of all students, including those from diverse racial, ethnic, linguistic, and ability backgrounds. Bondy and Tincani (2018) evaluated the effects of preprinted response cards on participation and correct responding for three elementary-aged students with autism spectrum disorder and intellectual disability. Students were recruited to participate because they participated infrequently during group lessons unless they received substantial prompting from their teacher. During a baseline condition, the teacher asked the students about the calendar and basic math operations, and they were given the opportunity to respond one at a time by raising their hands. Each student demonstrated low rates of participation and correct responding during baseline. Then, during intervention, students were given preprinted response card binders; each page in the binder contained pages with four picture symbols that were velcroed to each page. For example, the binder page in Figure 5.3 contained picture symbols for a lesson about the calendar. Students were taught to answer the teacher's questions in unison by removing the correct picture from the binder and holding it up for the teacher to see. Response cards substantially increased each student's participation and correct responding compared with hand-raising.

Response cards can be used across a variety of lesson content. For instance, a math teacher can present addition facts to students who can write the correct sums on their cards. A US history teacher can state major events during the

Figure 5.3 Sample response card page from a student binder for teacher question, 'What month is it?' Reprinted with permission from Bondy, A. H., & Tincani, M. (2018). Effects of response cards on students with autism spectrum disorder or intellectual disability. *Education and Training in Autism and Developmental Disabilities*, 53(1), 59–72.

American Revolution and ask students to write the correct year or location. A reading teacher can say vocabulary words and have students spell the words on their cards.

Figure 5.4 shows how a typical lesson is taught using response cards (see also Heward, 1994). First, you will need to identify a set of questions, such as math facts, history facts, or vocabulary words. It is a good idea to come up with at least 10–20 questions for each lesson. If you are using write-on response cards, the answers must be short enough to fit on the response cards. Then, you will present each question to the class, as you see on the left-hand side of Figure 5.4. Visual aids, including problems written on the whiteboard, are often helpful.

After you ask your question, you will allow students *wait-time* to think about and write answers on their response cards. The wait-time period should be as brief as possible (i.e., five seconds or less); however, difficult or new items may require additional wait-time (Tincani & Crozier, 2007). Following wait-time, you will present a cue for students to raise their cards and show their answers, such as, 'Cards up!' or 'Show me!' This way, you will be able to see all of your students' responses at the same time.

Next, you will immediately provide feedback on the majority of students' responses. As you see in Figure 5.4, feedback should include a praise

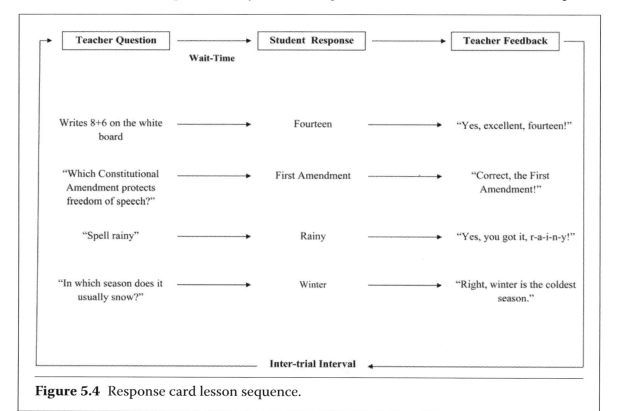

Figure 5.4 Response card lesson sequence.

statement followed by the correct answer. Feedback should be delivered as quickly as possible after students respond. Make note if there is a consistent error pattern among any students – this indicates that they are not learning the material at the same rate as the majority of the class and may need extra assistance.

Finally, *inter-trial interval* (ITI) is the time period between the teacher's feedback and the beginning of the next question. It is best to keep the inter-trial interval short in order to maximize your rate of ASR and minimize students' opportunity to engage in off-task behaviors (Carnine, 1976; Tincani et al., 2005). An inter-trial interval of three to five seconds should be sufficient.

Choral Responding

Choral responding, another way to increase ASR, occurs when students vocally respond in unison to teacher-presented questions (Haydon et al., 2009; Heward, 1994). Like response cards, choral responding increases ASR by allowing the entire class to participate. Students who chorally respond during instruction are more engaged and less likely to perform off-task behaviors.

> **Choral responding:** When students vocally respond in unison to teacher-presented questions.

Teaching with choral responding involves procedures similar to those of response card lessons. The teacher presents a question to the group, allows for wait-time, and then provides a signal for students to chorally respond, followed by feedback. Choral responding can be done with the whole class or by dividing students into smaller groups. The following guidelines will help you develop lessons with choral responding (see also Heward, 1994):

❏ Select a series of questions that require short responses (e.g., one to three words or numbers)

❏ Provide a clear cue for students to respond. For example, 'Tell me' or 'How many' followed by a hand signal. For new or more difficult material that requires longer wait-time pauses, a cue such as 'Get ready' may be helpful before you give students the cue to respond.

❏ Give students sufficient wait-time to formulate their answers before they respond (see Figure 5.4). One to three seconds is optimal, but new or more difficult questions may require additional wait-time.

❏ Provide feedback for the majority response.

❏ Occasionally call on individual students at random to verify correct responses.

Guided Notes

Guided notes: Handouts that guide a student through a lecture with standard cues and prepared space in which to write the key facts, concepts, and/or relationships.

Guided Notes are an effective approach to increase ASR for lessons involving lectures, particularly for students at the middle- and high-school levels. Heward (1994) defines guided notes as 'teacher-prepared handouts that guide a student through a lecture with standard cues and prepared space in which to write the key facts, concepts, and/or relationships' (p. 304). Guided notes provide students with an accurate record of the lecture, and are an effective tool to improve academic performance (Konrad et al., 2009). A sample guided notes page for a lesson on plants is found in Figure 5.5.

Guided notes are an effective classroom management and teaching tool in three important ways. First, they decrease off-task behaviors by engaging students in note-taking; students are less likely to perform off-task behaviors when they are focused on writing notes. Second, guided notes draw students' attention to salient information during the lecture. Third, because students are often poor note takers, guided notes provide a more accurate record of the lesson that can be used for study and review; this, in turn, improves performance on tests and quizzes.

Technology enables teachers to create guided notes easily. Guided notes for a lecture can be typed directly into any word processing program. Or, if you are using Microsoft PowerPoint or a similar app to present your lectures, you can copy and paste your slides into a word processing program, and then insert spaces to create guided notes. The author of this book uses this method to create guided notes for his students.

The following guidelines will help you develop guided notes for your lectures (see also Heward, 1994):

- ❏ Provide consistent cues, such as bullet points, asterisks, and lines, so that students know where to write.
- ❏ Vary the location where students have to fill in the blank. This will maintain their attention to the guided notes and the lecture.
- ❏ Don't make students write too little or too much. The amount students write will depend on their age, academic level, and writing skills. As you deliver the lecture, periodically check to make sure students are keeping up, but not writing in their notes so quickly or so little that they don't need to pay attention.
- ❏ Use follow-up activities with the guided notes, such as daily quizzes or peer tutoring activities, to ensure that students use the guided notes after they complete them.

Earth Science Guided Notes   Name:_____

Lesson 4: Basic Parts of a Plant

☐ _____

   - Absorb water and _____ from the soil.

   - Anchor the plant into the _____.

☐ Leaves

   - In the _____, the plant uses water and air to make it grow.

   - Leaves contain _____, a green pigment that helps the plant make food.

☐ _____

   - Stems hold the _____ of the plant.

   - Stems carry water and _____ to all parts of the plant.

☐ The _____ of the plant holds the stems.

☐ _____

   - Attract _____ and _____ to the plant by their color, sweet

     smell, or _____.

   - These animals help _____ the flower, or deliver pollen to the flower, which

     turns the flower into fruit.

☐ _____

   - Contain _____ which can grow into new plants.

   - _____ the seeds and holds them there until they are _____ to

     get out.

☐ _____

   - Are found inside the _____.

   - Carries a _____ plant and has nutrients so the new plant can _____.

Figure 5.5 Sample guided notes.

ACTIVITY

Develop a lesson to teach an academic skill using one of the high ASR methods we have discussed: response cards, choral responding, or guided notes. Within your lesson plan, identify the subject matter and the students' grade level. Then, write the lesson topic, the questions you will ask, how students are expected to respond, and how you will provide feedback for correct and incorrect responses. Use the guided form in Figure 5.6 to create the lesson plan.

High Active Student Responding (ASR) Lesson Plan

Subject: _____ *Grade level*: _____

Type of ASR strategy (circle one): Response Cards / Choral Responding / Guided Notes

☐ What is the lesson topic?

☐ What questions you will ask students?

☐ How students will be expected to respond?

☐ How will you provide feedback for correct and incorrect responses?

Figure 5.6 ASR lesson planning guide.

Brisk Instructional Pacing

Brisk instructional pacing: When the teacher moves quickly through the lesson's content, minimizing downtime, while giving students sufficient wait-time to answer questions.

Brisk instructional pacing means that you move quickly through the lesson's content, minimizing downtime, while giving students sufficient wait-time to answer questions. Brisk instructional pacing does not mean that you hurry or rush through the lesson, but rather that you go as quickly as possible while maintaining high rates of ASR. Brisk instructional pacing increases ASR by providing more opportunities for students to respond during the lesson (Carnine, 1976; Tincani & Crozier, 2007; Tincani et al., 2005). This can decrease off-task behavior because the more students are engaged during instruction, the less opportunity they have to perform problem behaviors.

Tincani and De Mers (2016) conducted a systematic review of research on instructional pacing. Among different parameters of instructional pacing they evaluated, they examined studies that compared the effects of brief and extended durations of ITI on students' rates of correct responding and their off-task behavior. They found that durations of ITI that were four seconds or less consistently increased students' correct responding and decreased their off-task behavior, compared to durations of ITI that were four seconds or more. Results of their review suggest that when teachers minimize instructional 'downtime' by reducing the duration of ITI, they increase their students' academic participation and lessen students' opportunities to perform off-task behaviors.

As we have seen, brisk instructional pacing can be incorporated into all of your lessons, including those with response cards and choral responding. These considerations will help you as you develop lessons with brisk instructional pacing.

Be organized. We learned about the importance of good classroom organization in effective behavior management in Chapter 4. Being an organized teacher will also facilitate brisk instructional pacing. For instance, having individual and class-wide activity schedules will produce briefer transitions, allowing more instructional time and higher rates of ASR. Just as important, making sure that all of your lesson prep is done before the lesson begins (e.g., all necessary materials are readily available to you, your teaching assistant(s), and your students), will help you teach briskly because you will not have to take time to ready instructional materials as you teach.

Minimize wait-time. As you can see in Figure 5.4, *wait-time* is the interval between the teacher's question and the student's response. You can control the wait-time interval by presenting a cue for students to respond after you ask a question (e.g., 'Tell me'). It may be helpful for you to count silently to yourself to control the duration of the wait-time interval. Generally, wait-time should be as brief as possible, three to five seconds or less, to promote high rates of ASR and minimize opportunities for problem behaviors. However, wait-time should be longer when (a) you are introducing new material; (b) you are asking a particularly challenging question; or (c) you are asking a question that requires a complex answer (e.g., more than one or two words) that requires thinking or collaboration among students to be answered correctly.

Minimize inter-trial intervals. Inter-trial interval is the time period between the teacher's feedback and the next question. You can think of inter-trial intervals as the downtime between learning opportunities within a lesson. Like wait-time, inter-trial intervals should be brief – one to three seconds – to increase ASR and decrease challenging behaviors. Unlike wait-time, inter-trial intervals do not usually need to be longer to accommodate new, challenging, or complex material. However, if students have additional questions between learning trials, it may be necessary to extend the inter-trial interval to accommodate those questions.

Technology to Enhance ASR in the Classroom

Thus far, we have explored inexpensive, 'low-tech' ways to promote ASR in the classroom. In the last several years, greater availability of portable technology, including powerful phones and tablet computers, has made 'high-tech' ways for promoting ASR more accessible for teachers and students. For instance, Kahoot! is a subscription app that allows teachers to present questions to a group of students in a game-based format via the computer. The questions can include true/false, multiple-choice, and/or type-in responses. Students log in and 'play' Kahoot using their phones, tablets, or laptop computers. The teacher can set a fixed time limit for students to answer each question, and students can compete with one another to earn points for correctly answering questions. Kahoot! provides immediate feedback to students on whether they made a correct or incorrect response and tracks each student's answers.

Considerations for whether a teacher should adopt Kahoot! or another high-tech student response system are similar to those for low-tech ASR methods. Like the low-tech methods we have discussed, systems such as Kahoot!

permit students to respond in unison to teacher-posed questions, and thus they can be a great way to increase ASR compared with traditional participation methods, like hand-raising. In addition, since high-tech ASR systems like Kahoot automatically collect data on students' responses, the teacher does not need to collect any additional data to keep track of students' progress.

There are also potential drawbacks of high-tech ASR methods that teachers must consider. Technology is not free, and each student will need access to their own device to participate. In addition, the teacher or school may need to pay a subscription fee to create ASR activities that students can access. While systems such as Kahoot! can automatically track students' responses, unlike response cards, the teacher cannot individually see each student's response, and thus they cannot provide individualized feedback or gauge how well all students are doing during the activity. Finally, though both low-tech and high-tech ASR methods require organization and planning, teachers must program each question into apps like Kahoot! in advance, so unlike response cards and choral responding, they cannot ask questions spontaneously, or pose clarifying questions on the fly.

Summary

Active student responding occurs when a student emits a detectable response to ongoing instruction. ASR increases students' academic engagement and lessens opportunities to engage in problem behaviors. Four ways to increase ASR are response cards, choral responding, guided notes, and brisk instructional pacing. Response cards can be made inexpensively and enable students to write or select the correct answer and show their cards to the teacher. Similarly, choral responding increases ASR by allowing all students in the class to respond in unison to teacher-posed questions. Guided notes are preprinted handouts with spaces for students to write critical information about a teacher's lecture. Brisk instructional pacing can be used with these and other instructional strategies to minimize downtime and increase rates of ASR. High-tech systems, such as the Kahoot! app, can be a great way to increase ASR in the classroom; however, cost and availability can be barriers to students' accessing these systems.

Key Terms

Active student responding – When a student emits a detectable response to ongoing instruction, such as saying, writing, or typing an answer.

Brisk instructional pacing – When the teacher moves quickly through the lesson's content, minimizing downtime, while giving students sufficient wait-time to answer questions.

Choral responding – When students vocally respond in unison to teacher-presented questions.

Guided notes – Handouts that guide a student through a lecture with standard cues and prepared space in which to write the key facts, concepts, and/or relationships.

Inter-trial interval – The time period of the teacher's feedback and the next teacher-posed question.

Response cards – Write-on or preprinted cards on which students write or select answers during teacher-directed lessons.

Wait-time – The interval between when the teacher asks a question and the student responds, usually controlled by a cue from the teacher.

CHAPTER 6

Classroom-Wide Behavior Support

Chapter Objectives

- Define the four basic principles of behavior that are critical in effective classroom management.

- Understand and implement seven classroom-wide behavior support strategies to prevent and reduce problem behaviors in your classroom.

DOI: 10.4324/9781003237228-6

This chapter focuses on secondary prevention in positive behavior support, classroom-based strategies to help ensure that low-level challenging behaviors do not become persistent problems. First, we will overview four key principles of behavior – positive reinforcement, negative reinforcement, punishment, and extinction – and how they affect appropriate and challenging behaviors in the classroom. Then, we will discuss seven important classroom-wide behavior support strategies that will help you become an effective classroom manager. The strategies are (a) contingent praise and attention; (b) behavior-specific praise; (c) teaching students to recruit teacher attention; (d) error correction; (e) publicly posting classroom rules and reinforcing rule following; (f) group contingencies; and (g) active supervision.

Basic Principles of Behavior in the Classroom

What are the basic principles of behavior? The word 'basic' implies simple; however, in this case, 'basic' means fundamental – principles of behavior that are common to all members of the human species, including students in your classroom. Educators focus a lot on how children are unique (and they certainly are). Even so, all children's behaviors are sensitive to four basic principles: positive reinforcement, negative reinforcement, punishment, and extinction. It is important to understand how these principles affect your students so that you can use them to promote learning and good behaviors in your classroom.

Reinforcement

Reinforcement: Any event following a behavior that increases the likelihood that the behavior will occur again.

Before we discuss the differences between positive and negative reinforcement, you should understand the general principle of *reinforcement*, which is any event following a behavior that increases the likelihood that the behavior will occur again (Cooper et al., 2020; Skinner, 1953). For example, while two of your students are quietly working, you say, 'I really like the way you two are working hard,' and, as a result, the students increase their time quietly working in the future.

Importantly, reinforcement is defined by its effect on behavior. If you praise a student for performing a particular behavior, but it does not increase the behavior's future occurrence, then praise is not reinforcement. A consequence is only reinforcement if it increases how much the behavior happens in the future. Therefore, what functions as reinforcement is individualized to the student, the behavior, and the situation. So, praise may function as reinforcement for one student's behavior, but not for another student's behavior. Similarly, praise might effectively reinforce a student's behavior of completing work assignments in science, but not her behavior of playing volleyball in gym class. Again, a consequence is defined as reinforcement only if it increases behavior.

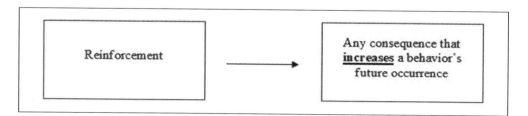

Positive reinforcement. Positive reinforcement occurs when you add something following a behavior which increases the likelihood that the behavior will occur again. Examples include praise and other forms of social recognition, tokens, money, tangible items, food, beverages, and preferred activities. From the student's perspective, positive reinforcement occurs when he performs a behavior, gets something, and consequently performs the behavior more often.

Positive reinforcement: When you add something following a behavior which increases the likelihood that the behavior will occur again.

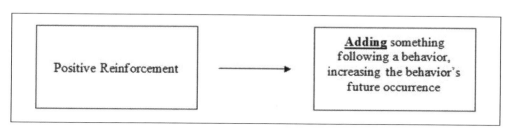

Behavior	Consequence	Effect
Student smiles	Classmate says, 'I like your smile.'	Student smiles more in the future
Student correctly solves geometry problem	Teacher writes, 'Correct!'	Student correctly solves more geometry problems in the future
Student screams	Teacher reprimands student	Student screams more in the future

A consequence functions as positive reinforcement only if it increases behavior. In the first example, the student's smiling is positively reinforced because it happens more frequently following their classmate's compliment. However, if the student smiled, their classmate complimented them, and they stopped smiling, this would not be positive reinforcement, as the behavior did not increase. Notice the consequence in the last example, a reprimand functions as positive reinforcement. In this case, when the student screams, their teacher reprimands them, and they scream more frequently in the future. Although the teacher did not intend for the reprimand to function as positive reinforcement because it increased the behavior's occurrence, the reprimand is positive reinforcement. This example shows that we cannot assume the function of a consequence unless we know its effect on behavior. Although we may presume that a reprimand will decrease behavior, as a form of attention, reprimands can actually reinforce students' problem behavior. We will learn more about how to determine what consequences are reinforcing problem behavior in Chapter 7.

Negative reinforcement. Negative reinforcement occurs when you remove something following a behavior which increases the likelihood that the behavior will occur again. For example, your student politely asks if she can take a short break from a difficult assignment, you grant her request, and, as a result, she asks for breaks during difficult assignments more frequently in the future. From the student's perspective, negative reinforcement occurs when she performs a behavior, escapes, or avoids something aversive, and subsequently performs the behavior more often.

> **Negative reinforcement**: When you remove something following a behavior which increases the likelihood that the behavior will occur again.

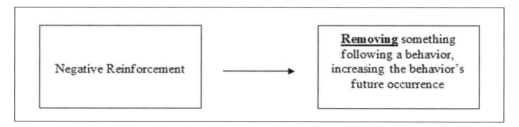

Behavior	Consequence	Effect
Student writes vocabulary word definitions	Teacher gives student a 15-minute break	Student writes more vocabulary word definitions in the future
Student completes all her homework	Teacher gives student a one-day homework pass	Student completes more homework assignments in the future
Student screams	Teacher sends student out of the classroom	Student screams more in the future

In each of the above examples, the student performs a behavior, the teacher removes something aversive, and the student performs the behavior more frequently in the future. In the first example, the student writes all her vocabulary definitions, the teacher provides a 15-minute break, which results in a temporary escape from her work, and the student writes more vocabulary definitions in the future. In the second example, the student completes her homework, and the teacher provides a homework pass, which results in a temporary escape from the aversive task of homework, and the student completes more homework in the future. In the final example, the student screams, the teacher sends them out of the classroom, which results in a temporary escape from the classroom (and academic demands), and the student screams more frequently in the future. In the last example, the teacher did not intend to reinforce the student's screaming by sending her out of the room, but because this consequence increased her behavior, we know it is negative reinforcement.

Both positive and negative reinforcement have one thing in common, they increase the future occurrence of behaviors. Negative reinforcement is sometimes confused with punishment, discussed later in this chapter, which has the opposite effect on behaviors.

ACTIVITY

Identify one academic, social, or other behavior and how you would increase the behavior using *positive* reinforcement. Then, identify another academic, social, or other behavior and how you would increase the behavior using *negative* reinforcement. In your responses, describe how you would tell whether your consequence is functioning as positive or negative reinforcement.

- Positive reinforcement:

  _____

  _____

  _____

  _____

  _____

  _____

  _____

- Negative reinforcement:

  _____

  _____

  _____

  _____

  _____

  _____

  _____

Discriminative Stimuli and Stimulus Control

A *discriminative stimulus*, abbreviated S^D, plays an important role in the process of reinforcement. An S^D is a stimulus, preceding a behavior, which signals that reinforcement is available for the behavior. S^Ds evoke behaviors that are followed by reinforcement. When a behavior occurs reliably in the presence of an S^D, but not in the presence of other stimuli, the behavior is under *stimulus control*.

Consider a student who is told by her teacher that she can ask for her tablet computer to play games, but only during the last ten minutes of class. When the clock reads 9:50 am (S^D), the student raises her hand to ask for her tablet (behavior), and the teacher gives her the tablet (reinforcement) (which type of reinforcement is it?). This process illustrates the *three-term contingency of behavior*, an S^D is presented, which evokes a behavior, that is followed by reinforcement. We know the behavior is under stimulus control when the student asks for her tablet during the last ten minutes of class, but not during other times when the teacher is unlikely to provide reinforcement.

> **Discriminative stimulus (S^D)**: A stimulus, preceding a behavior, which signals that reinforcement is available for the behavior. S^Ds evoke behaviors that are followed by reinforcement.
>
> **Stimulus control**: When a behavior occurs reliably in the presence of an S^D, but not in the presence of other stimuli.
>
> **Three-term contingency of behavior**: When an S^D is presented, which evokes a behavior, that is followed by reinforcement.

Three-term contingency		
Discriminative stimulus (S^D)	Behavior	Consequence
Clock reads 9:50 am	Student asks for tablet	Teacher gives her tablet

When a student's behavior does not occur in the presence of a desired S^D, we may need to add a supplemental S^D, a type of *prompt*, for the student to perform the behavior. A prompt is a supplemental S^D,

> **Prompt**: A supplemental discriminative stimulus (S^D), or other forms of assistance, to produce a desired behavior.

or other forms of assistance, to produce the desired behavior. In the previous example, if the student asks to use her tablet at inappropriate times, the teacher might prompt her at the beginning of class with this reminder, 'Remember, you can only ask for your tablet during the last ten minutes of class.' Or the teacher might write 9:50 am on an index card and place it on the student's desk as a prompt for her to ask for her tablet only during the last ten minutes of the period.

Punishment

Punishment: Any event following a behavior that decreases the likelihood that the behavior will occur in the future.

In contrast to reinforcement, *punishment* is any event following a behavior that decreases the likelihood that the behavior will occur in the future (Cooper et al; Skinner). For instance, a student in your classroom teases another student, you say, 'Stop that,' and, as a result, the student no longer teases other students.

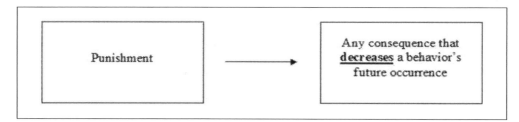

While punishment and negative reinforcement both involve aversive stimuli as consequences, with punishment, the student performs a behavior less frequently after receiving an aversive consequence. With negative reinforcement, a student performs a behavior more frequently by escaping or avoiding an aversive consequence.

As we learned in Chapter 3, the use of punishment as a classroom management technique accompanies undesirable side effects, including avoidance of environments where punishment occurs and disruptive behaviors toward the person administering punishment (Lee & Axelrod, 2005). Furthermore, while punishment can sometimes be effective in suppressing behaviors, it does not teach the student any new, appropriate behaviors to perform instead. Unfortunately, teachers may fall into the trap of overusing punishment because it produces an immediate, if temporary, cessation in the student's problem behavior. For these reasons, punishment should be considered a technique of last resort, and should always accompany reinforcement-based techniques, including the strategies we will explore in the next section.

Extinction

Extinction, our final basic principle of behavior, is like punishment in that it results in the student performing a behavior less often. However, extinction happens when you stop delivering a reinforcer for a behavior and consequently the student performs the behavior less frequently.

Extinction: When you stop delivering a reinforcer for a behavior and consequently the student performs the behavior less frequently.

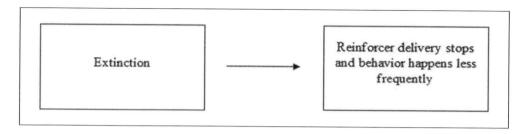

The following scenario illustrates extinction. Every day you praise a student for working quietly; he stays on-task as he completes his work. Therefore, praise functions as positive reinforcement. Then, you stop praising the student and subsequently he decreases the amount of time he spends on-task until he is no longer completing his assignments. So, by removing the reinforcer, praise, you have put the student's work behavior on extinction.

A common phenomenon often observed with extinction is *extinction burst*. This happens when you stop delivering a reinforcer for a behavior and the frequency and/or intensity of a behavior initially increases before it decreases. As we will discuss in Chapter 8, extinction burst can be a problem when you are using extinction as a behavior reduction procedure because it makes withholding the reinforcer more difficult.

Extinction burst: When you stop delivering a reinforcer for a behavior and the frequency and/or intensity of a behavior initially increases before it decreases.

Classroom-Wide Behavior Support Strategies

In this section, we will explore classroom-wide behavior support strategies that involve applications of the four basic principles of behavior.

Contingent Praise and Attention

Contingent praise and attention: The application of praise and other forms of attention only when the student has performed specific academic, social, or other good behaviors.

Contingent praise and attention is perhaps the most fundamental and important classroom management technique. It involves the application of praise and other forms of attention (e.g., smiles, pats on the back) only when the student has performed specific academic, social, or other good behaviors. Thus, contingent praise and attention is an application of positive reinforcement. At the same time, attention to off-task and other problem behaviors is minimized. Importantly, contingent praise and attention is most effective when delivered immediately after the target behavior occurs (Conroy et al., 2008).

In their seminal study, Hall et al. (1968) found that contingent praise and attention from teachers dramatically increased the study behaviors of six elementary-aged students who demonstrated low levels of study behaviors before intervention. Their simple procedure involved teachers immediately moving closer to students and providing a praise statement and gestural approval (e.g., pat on the back) when students were studying. Initially, a cue to praise students was provided to teachers by an observer; the cue was then faded.

Figure 6.1 shows the results of their study for one student, Ken. The conditions labeled baseline and reversal show Ken's percentage of studying without contingent praise and attention, and the conditions labeled reinforcement show Ken's percentage of studying with contingent praise and attention. As you can see, Ken's studying behavior considerably improved when his teacher gave him praise and attention for studying.

Contingent praise and attention is an example of positive reinforcement as a classroom management technique. It is also an example of extinction; as teachers reinforce appropriate behaviors, they minimize their attention to off-task, disruptive, and other inappropriate behaviors in the hope that these will decrease.

How much praise and attention should you use with your students? The question is hard to answer because, as we have discussed, reinforcement is individualized to the student, the behavior, and the situation. There are different recommendations on the best ratio of praise to negative interactions in the classroom. For example, Trussel (2008) recommends a 4:1 ratio of praise to

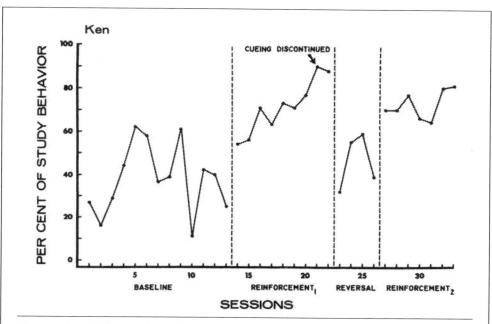

Figure 6.1 Effects of teacher attention on study behavior. Republished with permission of John Wiley & Sons from 'Effects of Teacher Attention on Study Behavior,' R.V. Hall, D. Lund, and D. Jackson, 1, 1968; permission conveyed through Copyright Clearance Center, Inc.

negative interactions, whereas Sugai (2008) recommends an 8:1 ratio of praise to negative interactions. Regardless, it is important that you provide more praise for appropriate behaviors than you provide reprimands and other forms of negative attention for problem behaviors.

Following these guidelines as you give students contingent praise and attention.

❏ Make a list of observable behaviors to reinforce with contingent praise and attention. For example, writing answers, talking quietly, taking turns, hand raising, or sharing.

❏ At first, it will be helpful to have another person, such as a teaching assistant or co-teacher, walk around the room and cue you when students are engaging in target behaviors to reinforce with contingent praise and attention. The cue could be a simple point toward the student who needs praise and attention. You can do the same for teaching assistants and other adults working in your classroom.

❏ To be most effective, praise and attention should be delivered immediately after the target behavior.

❏ Vary the ways in which you provide contingent praise and attention. Vary your praise statements (e.g., 'That's wonderful!' 'You are so smart.' 'What a hard worker you are!') and your gestures (e.g., pats on the back, thumbs up, winks, fist bumps). Don't just say, 'Good job' or repetitively issue the same praise statement.

❏ Minimize the attention you pay to problem behaviors. If you do, students will learn that the best way to get your attention is by being good.

❏ Try to maintain a ratio of at least 4:1 praise to negative statements. It may be helpful for you to count the number of times you praise students and the number of times you reprimand students during the class period to achieve this ratio.

Behavior-Specific Praise

Behavior-specific praise: Praise that provides information about the type, quality, or level of a student's behaviors.

As we learned in Chapter 3, *behavior-specific praise* (BSP) is when a teacher provides praise following a behavior by describing the behavior in specific terms Royer et al. (2019). BSP provides information about the type, quality, or level of a student's behaviors. We have discussed the importance of providing praise while minimizing attention to inappropriate behaviors. In addition to providing frequent and varied praise, it is beneficial to provide students with behavior-specific praise (Sutherland et al., 2000). Behavior-specific praise gives a student important feedback on her performance and how their academic and social behaviors are improving. Like all feedback, behavior-specific praise is most effective when delivered immediately after the target behavior.

ACTIVITY

Below are examples of behavior-specific praise. The parts that are in italics indicate information about the type, quality, or level of a student's behaviors. See if you can provide three behavior-specific praise examples of your own:

- 'Joel, I really liked the way you *raised your hand and waited patiently*.'
- 'Lupé, that was great *writing your name neatly*.'
- 'You *got all of your math problems correct*, Amy, excellent!'
- 'Rashad, *very nice sharing with your partner*.'

- _____.

- _____.

- _____.

Teaching Students to Recruit Teacher Attention

You have learned about the importance of teacher praise and attention; however, many students are not proficient at getting the teacher's attention when they need help with an assignment or they have done something that deserves recognition. Consequently, students may miss critical opportunities for teacher attention, including praise.

Teaching students to recruit teacher attention: Instructions, prompts, and reinforcement to help students independently get the teacher's attention when they have completed their work or need help from the teacher to complete their work.

Teaching students to recruit teacher attention involves instructions, prompts, and reinforcement to help students independently get the teacher's attention when they have completed their work or need help from the teacher to complete their work (Alber & Heward, 1997). Teaching students to recruit teacher attention has been shown to increase the frequency of teacher praise statements, as well as the number of work items and the accuracy of work items completed by students (Alber et al., 1999; Craft et al., 1998; Rouse et al., 2014).

Your students could benefit from learning to recruit teacher attention if (a) they do not independently raise their hands when they have a question or need help with assignments, or (b) they do not independently get your attention for feedback when they have completed a portion or all of their assignments. Craft et al. describe the following steps to teach students to recruit teacher attention:

Explain to students why it is important to recruit teacher attention. Reasons include that it helps students get their work done, improves their grades, and makes them feel good when they receive praise for doing their work completely and correctly.

Explain when and how often it is appropriate to ask for attention. You can use a think-aloud technique to illustrate when it is appropriate for students to seek attention (e.g., 'I'm finished with half of my problems, let's see how the teacher thinks I'm doing. Is she busy with other students? No. I'll raise my hand'). You can also provide specific instructions for when to seek attention, such as when the student's work is about halfway finished, when the student's work is totally finished, when the student doesn't understand instructions, or when the student is uncertain if he has answered a question or problem correctly. It is a good idea to

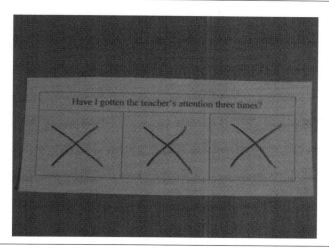

Figure 6.2 Visual prompting system for reminding a student to recruit teacher attention.

instruct the student to look and see if the teacher is not busy before he raises his hand.

Model and describe appropriate ways to get teacher attention. Students can be taught to raise their hands and wait to be recognized by the teacher or approach the teacher while she is at her desk (and not busy) to seek feedback. Phrases such as 'Is this right?' or 'How am I doing?' or 'I don't understand this?' can be modeled to demonstrate appropriate ways to solicit attention. Finally, you should give students a target for the number of times to recruit attention during a class period, such as three times.

Provide prompts for recruiting teacher attention. Prior to the beginning of class, you should provide a reminder to students about how, when, and how many times to seek the teacher's attention. A visual prompting system, such as you see in Figure 6.2, may be helpful in reminding students to recruit teacher attention. Each time the student recruits attention, he puts a check in the box. When all three boxes are checked, he knows that he has met his goal for the class period.

Positively reinforce recruiting teacher attention. At the end of the class period, review and provide behavior-specific feedback to the student on his recruiting teacher attention. If the student has met a specific goal (e.g., three times during one class period), you might provide a reward.

ACTIVITY

Identify a student you teach who is poor at recruiting teacher attention or think of a hypothetical student you might teach who is poor at recruiting teacher attention. Describe how you will teach the student to recruit teacher attention by explaining why it is important, when and how often to teacher recruit attention, and how to get the teacher's attention. Also, describe how you will prompt and reinforce the student for appropriately getting the teacher's attention.

_____

_____

_____

_____

_____

_____

_____

_____

_____

_____

_____

_____

_____

_____

_____

Error Correction

Your students will sometimes make mistakes while performing academic or social skills. It is important that you do not simply let mistakes go; if you do, students will practice errors and will have more difficulty mastering skills. *Error correction*

> **Error correction**: When a teacher systematically responds to an error to increase the student's accuracy with a skill.

occurs when a teacher systematically responds to an error to increase the student's accuracy with a skill. Error correction alone or in combination with other strategies has been shown to increase students' accuracy with spelling (Barbetta et al., 1993; Grskovic & Belfiore, 1996), geography facts (Barbetta & Heward, 1993), math (Maheady et al., 1987), purchasing retail items (Xin et al., 2005), labeling items (Townley-Cochran et al., 2017), and social skills (Lalli et al., 1991).

Successful error correction strategies share these key components that comprise an error correction sequence.

Immediate. The teacher performs error correction immediately after the student has made an error.

Modeling. The teacher models the correct response by saying it, writing it, or showing the student how to perform the skill correctly.

Active responding. The teacher has the student perform the correct response following the model.

Independent practice. The teacher gives the student an independent opportunity to perform the skill without the teacher's prompt. Typically, the teacher will require different responses before returning to the skill.

Figure 6.3 illustrates two error correction sequences for geography facts and spelling.

Posting Classroom Rules and Reinforcing Rule Following

Publicly posting classroom rules and reinforcing rule following is another critical strategy to promote good behaviors in your classroom (Conroy et al., 2008; Greenwood et al., 1974; Johnson et al., 1996). Publicly posted rules clearly communicate your expectations to students. Alter and Haydon (2017) reviewed research on teachers' use of rules in the classroom and noted two characteristics of effective rules across the studies: (a) teachers have procedures in place

Teacher: "What is the capitol of Washington?"	Teacher: "Spell 'fighter'."
Student: "Seattle."	Student: 'fitter'
Teacher (modeling correct response): "No. Tacoma"	Teacher models correct response by telling student to erase the first 't' and add 'gh'.
Student (actively responds to teacher model): "Tacoma."	Student (actively responds to teacher model): 'fighter'
Teacher, "Yes. Tacoma."	Teacher, "Good, 'fighter.'
Teacher asks a few different questions.	Teacher has the student spell several different words.
Teacher (provides opportunity for independent practice): "What is the capitol of Washington?"	Teacher (provides opportunity for independent practice): "Spell 'fighter'."
Student: "Tacoma"	Student: 'fighter'
Teacher: "Correct, Tacoma."	Teacher: "That's right. 'Fighter'."

Figure 6.3 Two error correction sequences for geography facts and spelling.

for teaching the rules to students; and (b) teachers apply contingencies for students following or violating the rules, including systems of positive reinforcement for rule following. Therefore, publicly posted rules are most effective when explicitly taught and combined with positive reinforcement, including behavior-specific praise. These guidelines will help you develop effective rules for your classroom:

❑ Make three to five positively stated rules. Positively stated means that the rules identify what students are supposed to do (e.g., 'Be respectful of your classmates') as opposed to what students are not supposed to do (e.g., 'Don't be disrespectful to your classmates'). Avoid writing negatively stated rules because they do not tell the student what to do and they encourage the use of punishment when rules are not followed.

❑ If possible, involve your students in the creation of classroom rules. This will encourage buy-in and will increase the likelihood that students will follow the rules. This will also facilitate classroom rules that have a good fit with students' cultural values and perspectives (see Chapter 2).

❑ Post your rules in a prominent location of the classroom (e.g., on the front board). Make the rules large enough that your students can see them from anywhere in your classroom.

Rules	Behavior-Specific Expectations
Respect your classmates.	Use polite words when you talk to other students. Share when you have extra of something. Be quiet when other students are working. Say hello to other students as they enter the classroom. Only touch other students in a friendly way (e.g. handshake, high five).
Always try your hardest.	Keep working until you have answered all the questions. Double check your work before you turn it in. If you are not sure about a problem, try your best to answer. If you feel frustrated, raise your hand to ask the teacher a question. If you finish early, find another activity to do.
Listen to the teacher.	Wait for the teacher to call on you before you talk. Listen carefully to the teacher's instructions before you begin. Ask the teacher before you leave the classroom. If you are unsure if it is OK to do something, ask the teacher first. When the teacher says, "Finished," put your work away and get ready for the next activity.

Figure 6.4 Examples of classroom rules and behavior-specific expectations.

❑ Spend at least five to ten minutes teaching each of the rules, including examples and non-examples of rule following. This could be done at the beginning of the class period. Examples of classroom rules and behavior-specific expectations are shown in Figure 6.4. You could also have students role play following the rules.

❑ Provide behavior-specific feedback and praise to students for following the rules. For instance, if one of your classroom rules is 'Listen to the teacher,' then an example of behavior-specific praise would be 'Josh, I like the way you finished your worksheet when I asked you, that's listening to the teacher.'

❑ Provide a reinforcer from your group-contingency system, discussed next, for students who follow the rules.

ACTIVITY

Write a set of three to five positively stated rules for your classroom or a hypothetical classroom. Describe where you will post the rules, how you will teach the rules, and how you will recognize students for following the rules.

_____

_____

_____

_____

_____

_____

_____

_____

_____

_____

_____

_____

_____

_____

_____

_____

_____

_____

_____

_____

Group Contingencies

Group contingencies are another effective way to prevent and reduce problem behaviors in the classroom (Stage & Quiroz, 1997). Group contingencies are special reinforcement systems in which part or all of the class must perform appropriate behaviors to earn a reward (Hulac & Benson, 2010). There are a number of ways to implement group contingencies in the classroom (Skinner et al., 2004); however, we will focus on two strategies: *independent group contingencies*, including classroom-wide token systems and check-in/check-out, and *dependent group contingencies*, such as the good behavior game.

Independent group contingencies. Independent group contingencies involve each student earning rewards for her own behaviors. *Classroom-wide token systems* are a type of independent group contingency in which the teacher makes the delivery of a reward contingent on each student earning a specified number of tokens, which are then exchanged for a backup reward. Classroom-wide token systems have important advantages as a reinforcement technique. First, they enable the teacher to arrange powerful rewards to reinforce students' appropriate behaviors. This is especially important because teacher praise and attention may not always be reinforcing for students' behaviors. Second, they enable the teacher to reinforce many different behaviors with tokens, and students learn that they must work over an extended period of time to earn the backup reward.

These guidelines will help you implement a classroom-wide token system:

❏ Select a group of reasonable rewards for students to earn with tokens. Rewards earned on a daily basis could include stickers, pencils, small edibles (e.g., mini candy bars), or brief activities (e.g., extra five minutes on the computer). Larger rewards earned on a weekly basis could include lunch with the teacher, a trip into the community, being class helper for a day, or a free pass from homework.

Group contingencies: Special reinforcement systems in which part or all of the class must perform appropriate behaviors to earn a reward.

Independent group contingencies: A type of group contingency in which each student earns rewards for their own behavior.

Dependent group contingencies: A type of group contingency in which students earn rewards as a group contingent upon some or all of the group's behavior.

- ❏ It is preferable to offer a limited selection of rewards and to have students choose which reward they will earn.
- ❏ When you introduce a classroom-wide token system, it is better to have students work for smaller rewards on a daily basis, rather than larger rewards on a weekly basis. For example, you could have students select a small reward to earn at the end of the class period if they have accumulated a small number of tokens (e.g., five). You can then progressively thin the schedule of reinforcement to have students earn more tokens over longer periods or work for larger rewards.
- ❏ Select your tokens. Tokens can be made from a variety of items, such as pennies or erasers. Tokens can also be tally marks on a piece of paper or stars drawn with a dry erase marker on laminated paper.
- ❏ Tokens can be placed on a token board, which can have a space for the student to write what she is earning (see Figure 6.5). This will serve as a reminder for the student about the contingency in effect.
- ❏ Select the number of tokens the student will earn for the reward. The number of tokens earned should correspond to the magnitude of the reward (e.g., sticker = five tokens; five minutes extra time at recess = 25 tokens; lunch with teacher = 75 tokens).
- ❏ Immediately deliver tokens for appropriate behaviors, including those specified by your classroom rules. Occasionally accompany the delivery of tokens with behavior-specific praise.
- ❏ When students have earned the requisite number of tokens, have them 'cash in' by handing you their tokens, or by counting the number of tally marks they have accumulated in exchange for the backup reward

Figure 6.5 Sample token board.

Check-in/check-out (CICO) is another application of independent group contingencies in the classroom that incorporates elements of the token system (Crone et al., 2010). With CICO, each student begins the day with a 'check-in' meeting with their teacher, teaching assistant, or another staff person, who manages their CICO system. During the initial meeting,

Check-in/check-out (CICO): A reinforcement system where students can earn points based on feedback about their behavior delivered via a daily behavior report card.

the manager reviews behavioral expectations with the student and provides them with a daily report card to complete for the day (see Figure 6.6). This report card specifies behaviors the student is expected to demonstrate throughout the day, which can be tied to established classroom or school-wide rules (Todd et al., 2008), and specifies a goal number of points for the student to earn that day. On the report card, each day is divided into feedback evaluation periods, which correspond with the student's class schedule. At the conclusion of each period, the student checks in with an adult, who gives them points based on their behavior during the period. Then, at the end of the day, the student has a 'check-out' meeting with their manager, who reviews their behavior for the day, tallies their points, and provides a reward based on whether they met their point goal for the day. The CICO report card in Figure 6.6 allows the student

Check-In / Check-Out Point Sheet

Name: _____

Date: _____ / _____ / _____

Goal: If I earn _____ points, I will get a reward!

Total points possible: _____ Total points earned: _____

2 = Awesome! 1 = Working on it 0 = Not there yet

Target Behaviors	Math	Social Studies	Special (Gym, Art, Library)	English	Lunch	Science
Be respectful (hands to self, be nice to classmates)	0 1 2	0 1 2	0 1 2	0 1 2	0 1 2	0 1 2
Work hard (listen to the teacher, complete all assigned work)	0 1 2	0 1 2	0 1 2	0 1 2	0 1 2	0 1 2
Be prepared (have all materials ready, start and finish on-time)	0 1 2	0 1 2	0 1 2	0 1 2	0 1 2	0 1 2
Rewards (pick one):	Choice of seat	Time with teacher	Board game	Surprise box	Extra tablet time	Class helper

Figure 6.6 Check-In/check-out point sheet

103

to choose from a menu of rewards. The completed sheet can then be sent home with the student for parents or other stakeholders in the home setting to review.

CICO has strong empirical support as a classroom-level PBS intervention for a variety of behaviors, settings, and students (Maggin et al., 2015; Wolf et al., 2016). One adaptation of CICO from the basic approach described above incorporates use of function-based supports (Campbell & Anderson, 2008) (see Chapter 8). That is, if we determine that a student's problem behavior is reinforced by a specific consequence, such as attention, we can arrange this consequence as a reinforcer for appropriate behavior in CICO. For example, if a student's disruptive behavior is maintained by attention from peers, we could allow the student to sit with peers of their choice during lunchtime if they meet their point goal in CICO. Alternatively, if a student's disruptive behavior is reinforced by escape from work, we could allow them to earn a break from work with CICO.

Dependent group contingencies. Dependent group contingencies involve students earning rewards as a group contingent upon some or all of the group's behavior. So, whether a student earns a reward is dependent not only on their performance but also on the performance of their classmates. The token systems we discussed in the last section can be adapted into dependent group contingencies. For instance, the class as a whole can choose a reward they want to work for, and the teacher can drop a marble in a jar each time any member of the class engages in one of the target positive behaviors. Then, if the class earns enough marbles by the end of the period or day, they will collectively earn their chosen reward.

The *good behavior game* is a different dependent group-contingency system in which the class is divided into two or more teams that compete for a reward based on their behavior. In the traditional version of the good behavior game, the team that displays the fewest problem behaviors earns a reward (Barrish et al., 1969; Dolan et al., 1993; Harris & Sherman, 1973; Rubow et al., 2018). In an adapted version of the game, the team that displays the most appropriate behaviors when they are 'caught being good' earns the reward (Joslyn et al., 2019).

Good behavior game: A type of dependent group contingency in which the class is divided into two teams that compete for a reward based upon which team displays the fewest problem behaviors.

To play the good behavior game with students in your classroom, you can:

❏ Identify a set of inappropriate behaviors that students should not perform in your classroom during the period, such as talking-out, aggression, cursing, stealing from other students, etc.

- ❏ Alternatively, identify a group of appropriate behaviors that the students should display.
- ❏ Divide the classroom into two or more groups.
- ❏ Identify a reward for the winning team.
- ❏ Explain to students that they will be competing against each other for which team has the fewest problem behaviors (or most good behaviors) and that the team with the fewest problem behaviors (or most good behaviors) will earn a reward. Describe each of the targeted behaviors to the class.
- ❏ Make a tally mark on the board every time a member of each team engages in one of the challenging behaviors (or good behaviors). You will have two sets of tally marks on the board for each team.
- ❏ The team with the fewest (or most) tally marks at the end of the period will earn the reward. If both teams have a low number of tally marks (e.g., less than five), or a high number of tally marks (e.g., more than 20), then both teams can earn the reward (Figure 6.7).

Randomization is one way to increase the effectiveness of both independent and dependent group-contingency systems (Hulac & Benson, 2010). Randomization makes group-contingency systems more motivating by having students guess about the contingency. To randomize your group-contingency system, you could (a) have students work for a secret reward contained in a 'surprise' box; (b) once students have earned the backup reward, spin a wheel, and have students earn whatever reward the wheel points to; or (c) in a dependent group-contingency system, select a small group of students in the class at random

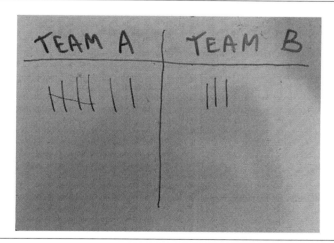

Figure 6.7 Tallying points with the good behavior game.

(e.g., by picking names out of a hat) and make the entire class's reward contingent on their behaviors. For example, if members of the randomly selected group complete their homework, then the entire class will earn a reward.

Active Supervision

Active supervision means the teacher actively looks around the classroom, moves around the classroom, and interacts with students to prevent instances of problem behaviors (Colvin et al., 1997; Depry & Sugai, 2002; Johnson-Gros et al., 2008). Active supervision is important because it enables the teacher to catch students being good and provide reminders about appropriate behaviors. When implementing active supervision, it is essential to give students behavior-specific praise for rule following and provide tokens or rewards from your group-contingency system when students engage in good behaviors.

> **Active supervision**: When the teacher actively looks around the classroom, moves around the classroom, and interacts with students to prevent instances of problem behaviors.

Precorrections are an important component of active supervision. Precorrections are prompts or reminders for students to engage in appropriate behaviors and to refrain from inappropriate behaviors. Importantly, precorrections are given to students before challenging behaviors occur and not after. Precorrections can be given to individual students or the whole class at the beginning of the period, or they can be given periodically throughout the period.

> **Precorrections**: Reminders for students to engage in appropriate behaviors and refrain from inappropriate behaviors.

Examples of precorrections could include:

- ❏ 'Remember, when you have a question, raise your hand and wait to be called on.'
- ❏ 'Listen to the teacher is a classroom rule, so listen for my instructions before you begin.'
- ❏ 'We use polite words in this class, so please refrain from saying mean words when you speak to your classmates.'

Summary

Four basic principles of behavior that are critical in classroom management are positive reinforcement, negative reinforcement, punishment, and extinction. Positive reinforcement occurs when you add something following a behavior which increases the likelihood that the behavior will occur again; negative reinforcement occurs when you remove something following a behavior which increases the likelihood that the behavior will occur again. When a behavior that is reinforced occurs reliably in the presence of a discriminative stimulus (S^D) and not in the presence of other stimuli, the behavior is under stimulus control. Punishment is any event following a behavior that decreases the likelihood that the behavior will occur in the future. Finally, extinction happens when you stop delivering a reinforcer for a behavior and consequently the student performs the behavior less frequently.

The chapter describes seven classroom-wide strategies for preventing challenging behaviors. Contingent praise and attention is the application of praise and attention only when the student has performed specific academic, social, or other good behaviors. Behavior-specific praise is a type of contingent praise in which the student receives specific feedback on her performance and how her academic and social behaviors are improving. All praise should be given immediately after appropriate behaviors occur. Teaching students to recruit teacher attention involves instructions, prompts, and reinforcement to help students independently get the teacher's attention when they have completed their work or need help from the teacher to complete their work. Error correction is when a teacher systematically responds to an error to increase the student's accuracy with a skill.

Publicly posting classroom rules and reinforcing rule following is an excellent way to communicate your behavioral expectations to students. Group contingencies are special reinforcement systems in which part or all of the class must perform appropriate behaviors to earn a reward. Classroom-wide token systems are a type of group contingency in which the teacher makes the delivery of a reward contingent on each student earning a specified number of tokens. Check-in/check-out is a different system where students receive daily behavior report cards with the opportunity to earn rewards. The good behavior game involves dividing the class into two teams that compete for a reward based upon which team displays the fewest problem behaviors. Finally, active supervision means the teacher actively looks around the classroom, moves around the classroom, and interacts with students to prevent instances of problem behaviors. Precorrections are an essential part of active supervision in which students are given reminders to engage in appropriate behaviors and refrain from inappropriate behaviors.

Key Terms

Active supervision – When the teacher actively looks around the classroom, moves around the classroom, and interacts with students to prevent instances of problem behaviors.

Behavior-specific praise – Praise that provides information about the type, quality, or level of a student's behaviors.

Check-in/check-out (CICO) – A reinforcement system where students can earn points based on feedback about their behavior delivered via a daily behavior report card.

Classroom-wide token systems – A type of independent group contingency in which the teacher makes the delivery of a reward contingent on each student earning a specified number of tokens, which are then exchanged for a backup reward.

Contingent praise and attention – The application of praise and other forms of attention only when the student has performed specific academic, social, or other good behaviors.

Dependent group contingencies – A type of group contingency in which students earn rewards as a group contingent upon some or all of the group's behavior.

Discriminative stimulus (S^D) – A stimulus, preceding a behavior, which signals that reinforcement is available for the behavior. S^Ds evoke behaviors that are followed by reinforcement.

Error correction – When a teacher systematically responds to an error to increase the student's accuracy with a skill.

Extinction – When you stop delivering a reinforcer for a behavior and consequently the student performs the behavior less frequently.

Extinction burst – When you stop delivering a reinforcer for a behavior and the frequency and/or intensity of a behavior initially increases before it decreases.

Good behavior game – A type of dependent group contingency in which the class is divided into two teams that compete for a reward based upon which team displays the fewest problem behaviors.

Group contingencies – Special reinforcement systems in which part or all of the class must perform appropriate behaviors to earn a reward.

Independent group contingencies – A type of group contingency in which each student earning rewards for her own behaviors.

Negative reinforcement – When you remove something following a behavior which increases the likelihood that the behavior will occur again.

Positive reinforcement – When you add something following a behavior which increases the likelihood that the behavior will occur again.

Precorrections – Reminders for students to engage in appropriate behaviors and refrain from inappropriate behaviors.

Prompt – A supplemental discriminative stimulus (S^D), or other forms of assistance, to produce a desired behavior.

Punishment – Any event following a behavior that decreases the likelihood that the behavior will occur in the future.

Reinforcement – Any event following a behavior that increases the likelihood that the behavior will occur again.

Stimulus control – When a behavior occurs reliably in the presence of an S^D, but not in the presence of other stimuli.

Teaching students to recruit teacher attention – Instructions, prompts, and reinforcement to help students independently get the teacher's attention when they have completed their work or need help from the teacher to complete their work.

Three-term contingency of behavior – When S^D is presented, which evokes a behavior, that is followed by reinforcement.

CHAPTER 7

Functional Behavioral Assessment

Chapter Objectives

- Define functional behavioral assessment (FBA) and describe why educators should conduct FBA.

- Identify the environmental reasons why students engage in challenging behaviors.

- Understand the three steps for conducting an FBA.

- Describe how the process of FBA informs behavior intervention programming.

DOI: 10.4324/9781003237228-7

Some students will require individualized, function-based interventions to reduce their chronic challenging behaviors. In this chapter, you will learn how to conduct an FBA to identify why students engage in difficult behaviors. We will explore the variables that lead to challenging behaviors, namely, motivating operations, antecedents, and consequences. We will then discuss methods for conducting an FBA, including indirect assessment, direct assessment, and functional analysis.

What is Functional Behavioral Assessment and Why Do We Do It?

Functional behavioral assessment (FBA) is a collection of strategies to identify the environmental reasons why students engage in challenging behaviors for the purpose of developing effective interventions (Alberto et al., 2020; Heron & Harris, 2001). The environmental reasons for challenging behaviors are often found in the classroom. For example, a student engages in problem behaviors to escape or avoid a classroom activity that he finds aversive. In Chapter 3, we discussed alterable variables, which are things the teacher can control to change student learning and behavior (Bloom, 1980; Heward, 2003). FBA guides us toward manipulating the right alterable variables to prevent and reduce problem behaviors in the classroom.

Therefore, if the student's FBA tells us that he engages in problem behaviors to escape or avoid an aversive activity, we could offer him a choice of activities, or we could teach him a more appropriate way to escape, such as by asking for a break or by requesting to do an alternate activity. We will discuss function-based intervention strategies in Chapter 8.

FBA is an essential part of developing a behavior intervention program (BIP), a written plan that describes procedures to prevent and reduce a student's challenging behaviors. Children with disabilities who engage in challenging behaviors that interfere with learning should receive individualized interventions based on positive behavior support. Specifically, when developing a student's individualized educational program, the team must:

> In the case of a child whose behavior impedes the child's learning or that of others, consider the use of *positive behavioral interventions and supports*, and other strategies, to address that behavior. (Individuals with Disabilities Education Improvement Act of 2004, H.R. 1350, Sec. 300.324(a)(2)(i))

BIPs that are informed by data collected from an FBA are more likely to be successful than BIPs that are not. This is because non-function-based interventions may not address the reasons why students engage in problem behaviors (Carter & Horner, 2007, 2009). For instance, if a student engages in destructive behaviors to escape from aversive classroom activities, we could use classroom rules, behavior-specific praise, and a group contingency system to teach appropriate behaviors (see Chapter 6); however, even with these interventions, the student will likely continue to be disruptive until we implement strategies to address the behavior's functions. Specifically, we could make classroom activities less aversive, or we could teach her more appropriate ways to seek escape. If disruption is reinforced by teacher attention, we could teach her more appropriate ways to seek teacher attention or provide her with more attention on a non-contingent basis.

Why Do Students Engage in Challenging Behaviors?

Challenging behaviors can seem like they come from nowhere, however, there are almost always specific environmental reasons why students engage in these behaviors. Next, we will explore the three environmental variables that maintain the most difficult behaviors. The environmental variables are motivating operations, triggering antecedents, and reinforcing consequences.

Motivating Operations

Motivating operations (MOs) alter the momentary value of reinforcers and the frequency of behaviors associated with those reinforcers (Laraway et al., 2003). For example, if a child is deprived of food for a period of time (MO), then food will become momentarily more reinforcing,

> **Motivating operations (MOs)**: Events that alter the momentary value of reinforcers and the frequency of behaviors associated with those reinforcers.

and behaviors associated with producing food (e.g., asking for a snack) will increase in frequency. In a different example, if a child becomes sick from a virus (MO), then escape-maintained behaviors may be momentarily more reinforcing. If she is presented with an assignment she doesn't like, she may, pinch, hit, or engage in other disruptive behaviors that result in escape from the assignment.

In Chapter 6 we learned about the three-term contingency, in which a discriminative stimulus (S^D) evokes a behavior, which is followed by reinforcement. The MO creates a four-term contingency, as you see in the examples below:

Four-term contingency			
Motivating operation	Discriminative stimulus	Behavior	Consequence
Food deprivation	Teacher at snack table	'Can I have a snack?'	Teacher gives snack (positive reinforcement)
Sickness from virus	Teacher presents work	Disruptive behaviors	Teacher removes work (negative reinforcement)

Importantly, MOs are often temporally distant from the behaviors they affect (Ray & Watson, 2001). This means that a relevant MO could happen hours before the student engages in challenging behaviors. For instance, when a child has had a typical night of sleep (i.e., eight hours), he might have few problem behaviors during school. However, a child's sleep deprivation the night before may serve as an MO for difficult behaviors throughout the school day, as you see in the example below. In this case, the MO, sleep deprivation, increases the reinforcing value of escape from work. Consequently, disruptive behaviors that result in escape are more likely when work is presented to the student. The temporally distant nature of some MOs presents a challenge to accurately identifying them in an FBA. Often, it is necessary to communicate with parents and staff in other settings to determine the presence of temporally distant MOs.

Four-term contingency			
Motivating operation	Discriminative stimulus	Behavior	Consequence
None	Teacher presents work	Student does work	Good grades, praise (positive reinforcement)
Sleep deprivation	Teacher presents work	Disruptive behaviors	Student is sent to office, avoids work (negative reinforcement)

Common examples of MOs that affect challenging behaviors are:

- ❏ Difficulty with the morning routine (e.g., getting up late, missing the bus)
- ❏ Arguments before school
- ❏ Arguments in another class
- ❏ Medication change
- ❏ Illness
- ❏ Sleep deprivation
- ❏ Change in family members present in the home setting

❏ Traumatic event at home
❏ Lack of attention from staff or peers
❏ Presence or absence of a specific staff person
❏ Presence or absence of a specific classmate
❏ Unpredictable schedule
❏ Loss of a preferred activity
❏ Disorganized transitions

Antecedents

Discriminative stimuli (Chapter 6), also known as *antecedents*, are stimuli that evoke or trigger challenging behaviors. Often, antecedents involve the presentation of difficult tasks, unclear instruc-

> **Antecedents**: Stimuli that trigger challenging behaviors, also known as discriminative stimuli (S^Ds).

tions, or the presence of non-preferred people. In the presence of these stimuli, the student may engage in disruptive behaviors to escape from or avoid them. For instance, the teacher gives the student a hard assignment, he hits another student, and then he is sent out of the classroom (and thus the demand is terminated). Antecedents also involve the presentation of preferred stimuli, such as preferred food and drink, preferred activities, and preferred people. In the presence of these stimuli, the student will engage in challenging behaviors to obtain them. For example, a teacher places a container of juice on the table and the student screams so that she will pour him a cup.

Reinforcing Consequences

As we learned in Chapter 6, reinforcement is any event following a behavior that increases the likelihood that the behavior will occur again. Positive reinforcement happens when you add something following a behavior which increases the likelihood that the behavior will occur again. For instance, one student pinches another student to get a toy; she takes the toy, and consequently she pinches more often in the future. Negative reinforcement happens when you remove something following a behavior which increases the likelihood that the behavior will occur again. For example, a student screams when the teacher presents a demand, the teacher removes the demand, and consequently the student screams more frequently to escape or avoid demands in the future.

The diagrams in Figure 7.1 show how MOs, antecedents, positive reinforcement, and negative reinforcement control challenging behaviors. The first two

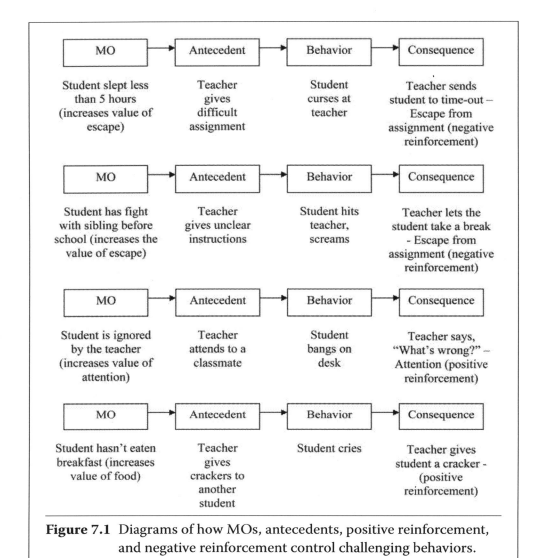

Figure 7.1 Diagrams of how MOs, antecedents, positive reinforcement, and negative reinforcement control challenging behaviors.

examples depict behaviors maintained by negative reinforcement; the next two examples depict behaviors maintained by positive reinforcement.

It is important to note that well-intentioned consequences can actually strengthen problem behaviors. For example, the second diagram in Figure 6.1 shows the teacher giving the student a break after the student hits and screams in the presence of a difficult assignment. Presumably, the teacher wants to let the student 'cool down' until he is ready for the assignment; however, the teacher is inadvertently reinforcing these problem behaviors by allowing the student to escape. It is therefore critical to understand the functions of problem behaviors before you develop interventions.

ACTIVITY

Below are two sets of boxes. Beneath the boxes, identify hypothetical MOs, antecedents, and consequences maintaining two different problem behaviors.

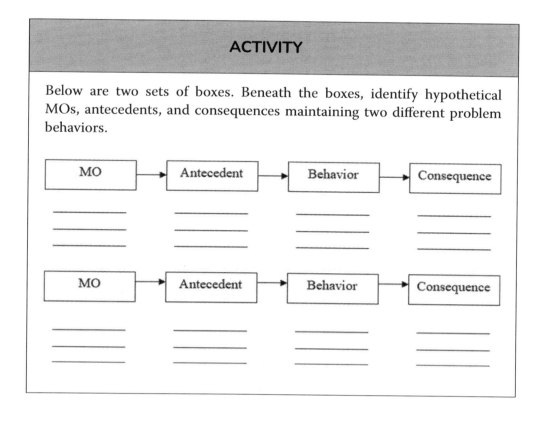

Conducting FBA

There are five steps in the FBA process (Tincani et al., 2018). These are 1) determine whether an FBA is necessary; and, if so, 2) convene the FBA team; 3) define the problem behaviors; 4) gather information; and 5) form hypothesis statements.

Step 1: Determine Whether an FBA Is Necessary

PBS emphasizes prevention as a key feature (Carr et al., 2002). Therefore, to this point in the book, we have focused on preventative interventions at the school- and classroom-wide levels. For most students, these strategies will be sufficient to prevent low-level challenging behaviors from becoming persistent issues that interfere with learning. However, even if teachers promote high rates of active student response, are very organized, and implement solid classroom-level management techniques, they will still encounter a small group of students for whom these measures are insufficient to prevent serious behavioral issues (Horner & Sugai, 2015). If a teacher is supporting a population of students who are prone to behavioral challenges, including students with disabilities, there may be more than a few students in their classrooms with serious problem behaviors.

When a student displays challenging behaviors that are disruptive to the student and others in the classroom, and stressful and time-consuming for the teacher, we may be tempted to immediately devise an individualized BIP to eliminate the behaviors. However, in determining whether an FBA and BIP are necessary, we should first ask, how well is the teacher implementing the classroom-level strategies described in the previous chapters of this book? In many cases, bolstering the teacher's implementation of classroom-level supports can eliminate seemingly intractable behavior problems, or reduce them to manageable levels, and prevent similar problems from creeping up in the future.

In other cases, a student's problem behavior may be immune to group-level interventions, or the behavior may be so disruptive or dangerous that it requires an immediate, individualized plan. As we discussed, if the student has an IEP and displays serious problem behaviors that impede their learning or others' learning, IDEA requires us to implement positive behavioral interventions and supports. Conducting an FBA is the first step in designing an effective BIP that will help the student and others around them.

Step 2: Convene the FBA Team

Once we have determined that an FBA and BIP are necessary, the next step is to convene the FBA team. Stakeholder input is a key feature of PBS (Carr et al., 2002). Therefore, we want to include individuals who know the student and the circumstances or their behavior in order to gather accurate information that will later inform the BIP. Team members can include, but are not limited to, parents, siblings, teachers, paraprofessionals, job coaches, counselors, psychologists, speech-language pathologists, and others who know the student. As we learned in Chapter 2, the input of family members is especially important for culturally and linguistically diverse students, so that our intervention strategies will have a good contextual fit with students' and families' cultural values and identities.

The team should include at least one member with expertise in conducting FBA (Tincani et al., 2018). This is because FBA strategies and data interpretation techniques often require specific expertise and training. Also, when we later

> **Board-certified behavior analyst (BCBA)**: A related-service provider with expertise in FBA and applied behavior analysis strategies.

develop the BIP, having an expert member of the team will help ensure the plan is technically sound and effective (Benazzi et al., 2006). Often, a *board-certified behavior analyst* (BCBA), a related-service provider with expertise in FBA and applied behavior analysis strategies, is best suited to provide technical support throughout the FBA process.

Step 3: Define the Problem Behaviors

The next step in conducting an FBA is to define the problem behaviors. One way to accomplish this is to talk with people who spend time with the student – teaching assistants, other school staff, and parents – and ask them to tell you what the problem behavior looks like and where it is most likely to occur. You can observe the student in the classroom or other settings to verify the presence and form of target responses. It will be helpful for you to ask if there are any specific routines (e.g., times of day, class periods, activities) in which problem behaviors are more likely. This will give you a clear picture of the behaviors and will focus your assessment efforts on the daily routines where difficulties are most likely. Some FBA questionnaires and rating scales, discussed in the next section, include specific questions about challenging behavior definitions and problematic daily routines.

It is critical to define problem behaviors in objective and observable terms (Scott et al., 2008). This means that you define each behavior in a clear and precise way so that you and others can measure it. Examples of behaviors that are not defined in objective and measurable terms include 'disruption,' 'frustration,' 'anger,' and 'disrespect.' Objective and observable definitions of these behaviors could be 'hitting and screaming,' 'tearing work materials,' 'pounding the desk,' and 'cursing.' The more specifically you write your definitions, the better.

ACTIVITY

In the table below, the left column contains descriptions of problem behaviors that are not objective and observable. The right-hand column contains revised definitions that are observable and measurable. For the last four examples, write in your own behavior definitions in observable and objective terms.

Non-objective, non-observable behaviors	Objective, observable behaviors
Tantrum	Screaming loudly, destroying work materials
Insubordinate	Refusing to follow teacher instructions, talking back
Meltdown	Falling to the floor, ponding floor, crying
Impulsive	Getting out of seat, calling out
Defiant	
Rude	
Inattentive	
Outburst	

Step 4: Gather Information

Once you have defined the problem behaviors, the next step is to gather information to form hypotheses about environmental variables that support the behaviors. There are many different methods to gather information for the FBA. These can be classified into three types: *indirect assessment, direct assessment,* and *functional analysis* (Tincani et al., 2018). We will explore the procedures, advantages, and disadvantages associated with each.

Indirect assessment: Interviewing people who know the student to gather information about variables maintaining problem behaviors.

Direct assessment: Observing the student in settings where problem behaviors occur and collecting data to discover patterns between antecedents, behaviors, and consequences.

Functional analysis: Experimental manipulation of variables thought to maintain challenging behaviors for the purpose of identifying behavior functions.

Indirect assessment. Indirect assessment involves interviewing people who know the student to gather information about variables maintaining problem behaviors. Indirect assessment can be done informally by asking questions about potential behavior functions. It is not recommended that you rely exclusively on informal interview data for the FBA because what you learn is likely to be subjective, biased, or to omit important information about the target responses and their functions.

Formal indirect assessments are questionnaires and rating scales to systematically identify behavior functions. Formal indirect assessments have three advantages as information-gathering tools. First, they provide structure to the process and guide the interviewer through questions that seek to identify a number of maintaining variables. Second, they allow the interviewer to gather information from multiple individuals. Finally, they are relatively easy and convenient to implement, particularly those assessments that involve rating scales that can be completed independently in a short period of time.

Table 7.1 shows five formal indirect assessment tools. The first two instruments, the Functional Assessment Checklist for Teachers and Staff (FACTS) (March et al., 2000) and the Functional Assessment Interview (O'Neill et al., 2015) are semi-structured interviews that seek to identify setting events (MOs), antecedents, reinforcing consequences, and other variables relevant to problem behaviors (e.g., student's medical history, previous interventions, communication skills). Semi-structured interviews provide comprehensive information that enables the evaluator to form hypothesis statements about variables

TABLE 7.1

Indirect FBA assessments

Instrument	Authors/date	Type of assessment	Procedures
Functional Assessment Checklist for Teachers and Staff (FACTS)	March, Horner, Lewis-Palmer, Brown, Crone, Todd, & Carr (2000)	Semi-structured interview	Two-part interview to identify problem behaviors, routines in which problem behaviors are most likely, and maintaining variables, including setting events (MOs), antecedents, and consequences. Concludes with a summary of problem behavior functions. Administered to teachers, staff, parents, or others who know the student
Functional Assessment Interview	O'Neill, Albin, Storey, Horner, & Sprague (2015)	Semi-structured interview	Interview with 11 sections of questions to identify setting events (MOs), antecedents, consequences, communication skills, and previous interventions. Designed to be used with Functional Assessment Observation.
Functional Assessment Screening Tool (FAST)	Iwata & DeLeon (2005)	Semi-structured interview and rating scale	Includes 16 yes/no questions to identify consequences maintaining problem behaviors. Intended as a screening tool to guide functional analysis.
Motivation Assessment Scale (MAS)	Durand & Crimmins (1988).	Rating scale	Contains 16 Likert scale questions to identify consequences maintaining problem behaviors.
Questions About Behavioral Function (QABF)	Paclawskyj, T. R., Matson, J. L., Rush, K. S., Smalls, Y., & Vollmer, T. R. (2000)	Rating scale	Uses 25 Likert scale questions to determine consequences maintaining problem behaviors.

related to problem responses. However, semi-structured interviews may take some time to complete, particularly if they contain a large number of items (e.g., Horner et al.) and are administered to several persons.

In contrast, the next three assessments in Table 7.1, the Functional Assessment Screening Tool (FAST) (Iwata & DeLeon, 2005), Motivation

Assessment Scale (MAS) (Durand & Crimmins, 1988), and Questions About Behavioral Function (QABF) (Paclawskyj et al., 2000), are rating scales in which the interviewee rates the likelihood of problem behaviors occurring in the presence of various consequences. Ranging from 16 to 25 items, these instruments require less time to complete than semi-structured interviews. However, rating scales yield limited information about behavior functions; most identify consequences reinforcing problem behaviors but do not yield information about problem routines, MOs, or triggering antecedents.

Indirect assessment provides convenient information about behavior functions; however, indirect assessment is inherently subjective because it evaluates team members' perceptions of why problem behaviors occur, which may or may not reflect actual maintaining variables (Tincani et al., 2018). A more accurate approach is to combine indirect assessment with direct assessment, discussed next.

Direct assessment. Direct assessment means observing the student in settings where problem behaviors occur and collecting data to discover patterns between antecedents, behaviors, and consequences. Direct assessment is potentially more accurate than indirect assessment because it involves direct confirmation of patterns between behaviors and environmental events. Direct assessment is potentially more effortful and time-consuming than indirect assessment, though it yields more reliable information.

Scatter plot: A type of FBA direct assessment that uses a grid to identify patterns in problem behaviors across time.

ABC assessment: A type of FBA direct assessment in which the observer records every instance of the challenging behavior, including the time the behavior occurred, what happened just before the behavior, and what happened just after the behavior.

There are myriad ways to perform direct assessment, including *scatter plots* (Touchette et al., 1985), *ABC assessment* (Bijou et al., 1968), and *the Functional Assessment Observation* (O'Neill et al., 2015). Scatter plots involve creating a grid to identify patterns in problem behaviors across time. The vertical axis of the grid segments time into hours, half hours, quarter hours, or any time unit appropriate to the student's schedule. The horizontal access segments the grid into successive days. Each box on the grid is shaded when the problem behavior occurs during the interval or left un-shaded when the problem behavior does not occur during the interval. Partial shading indicates that the behavior happened one to four, full shading indicates that the behavior happened five or more times. At the end of the week, the scatter plot can be visually inspected to determine if there are consistent patterns between times of day and the occurrence of problem responses. Scatter plots do not identify specific antecedents and consequences; however, they lead the assessor to events that reliably coincide with problem behavior episodes.

Figure 7.2 shows a hypothetical scatter plot with data. The shaded areas indicate intervals in which hitting occurred. The data suggest that hitting most often happened between 2:00 pm and 3:00 pm. Thus, we can conclude that whatever activities were happening between 2:00 pm and 3:00 pm are related to hitting. Therefore, our interventions should focus on modifying these activities so that they are less likely to evoke the student's hitting.

In ABC assessment, the observer records every instance of the challenging behavior, including the time the behavior occurred, what happened just before the behavior, and what happened just after the behavior. The purpose of ABC assessment is to establish patterns of antecedents and consequences over time to determine behavioral functions (see Figure 7.3). For example, after several days of observation if transitions consistently precede aggression, it is likely that these are antecedents for aggression. Similarly, if being redirected by the teacher is a reliable consequence of aggression, it is probably reinforcing aggression. Understanding the antecedents and reinforcing consequences for problem behaviors allows us to develop interventions to modify them.

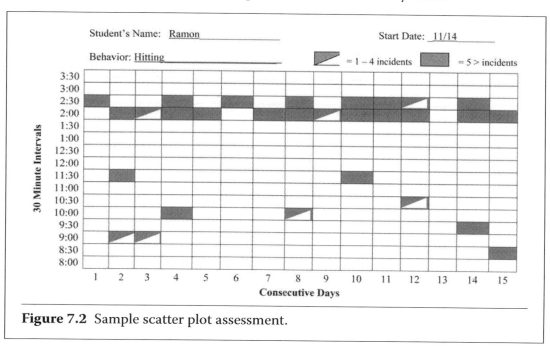

Figure 7.2 Sample scatter plot assessment.

Student: Lisa		Observer: Ms. Ramirez	Date: 9/17
Time begin: 8:00		Time end: 3:00	
Time	**Antecedent**	**Behavior**	**Consequence**
8:56 AM	Transition	Pinching	Redirected by teacher
9:29 AM	Transition	Hitting	Redirected by teacher
10:48 AM	Worksheet	Tearing	Time-out

Figure 7.3 Sample ABC assessment.

ABC checklist: A variation of the ABC assessment with predefined antecedents, behaviors, and consequences.

The *ABC checklist* is a variation of ABC assessment. The ABC checklist contains predefined antecedents, behaviors, and consequences, and the observer checks off each that corresponds with a specific behavioral episode (see Figure 7.4) (Tincani et al., 2018). Like the standard ABC assessment, the goal of the ABC checklist is to identify patterns between behaviors, antecedents, and consequences over time. Unlike narrative data collection in the standard ABC assessment, the ABC checklist yields quantitative data that can be compared across different observers, which adds a degree of objectivity to the assessment. It also draws the observer's attention to specific antecedents, behaviors, and consequences, and enables the observer to record multiple antecedents, behaviors, and consequences simultaneously. However, since the ABC checklist limits the number of antecedents, behaviors, and consequences recorded to those listed on the form, it is possible that observers may not record additional variables that are not on the form.

Finally, the Functional Assessment Observation is a structured direct assessment tool that combines elements of scatter plot assessment and ABC assessment. The Functional Assessment Observation is intended to be used with the Functional Assessment Interview to confirm behavioral functions (O'Neil et al., 2015). The observer collects data on antecedents and consequences for challenging behaviors within a grid, which enables the observer to establish patterns between times of day, antecedents, consequences, and problem behaviors.

Student:	Jamie			
Date/Time/Initial	Act/Location	Antecedent	Behavior	Consequence
Date: 11/4 Time: 10:38 Initial: MT	Activity: Science Location: Room 118	☐ Teacher delivered demand ☐ Teacher ended preferred activity ☐ Teacher delivered social attention ☒ Teacher attention diverted ☐ Peer within close proximity ☐ Requested assistance ☐ Engaged in leisure activity ☐ Alone, doing nothing ☐ Transitioning between locations ☐ Other: _____	☐ Aggression ☐ Out-of-seat ☐ Disruption ☒ Destroying ☐ Off-task ☐ Self biting fingertips ☐ Self pinching ☐ Disruption Define: _____ ☐ Out of seat ☐ Mouthing ☐ Other: _____	☐ Behavior ignored ☐ Redirected ☒ Reprimanded ☒ Provided with assistance ☐ Provided with item(s): _____ ☐ Escaped task ☐ Continued with task ☐ Other: _____

Figure 7.4 An example of a structured ABC assessment.

Functional analysis. Functional analysis is the experimental manipulation of variables thought to maintain challenging behaviors (Iwata et al., 1982/1994). Unlike direct assessment, the professional conducting functional analysis sets up conditions – or experimental analogs – in which the problem behavior is likely to occur. For example, if the behavior is thought to be maintained by escape from task demands, the experimenter will give the student a demanding task and will remove the task when the student performs the challenging behavior. If the behavior occurs under these circumstances, then it is probably maintained by escape from task demands. Typically, the professional alternates different conditions, including escape, attention, tangible reinforcement, or play (control condition) to see if a differentially higher rate of behavior occurs in one or more conditions.

Functional analysis: Experimental manipulation of variables thought to maintain challenging behaviors for the purpose of identifying behavior functions.

There are different formats to conduct functional analysis, including extended and brief analyses (Tincani et al., 1999) and classroom-based assessments (Ellis & Magee, 1999). The trial-based functional analysis (TBFA) is a brief functional analysis technique that is conducted in a classroom or other naturalistic setting where the student typically engages in challenging behavior (Rispoli et al., 2014). Functional analysis is the most resource and time intensive of the FBA methods we have discussed and should only be conducted by highly trained professionals, such as a BCBA with expertise and experience in conducting FA. This is because there are risks associated with setting up conditions where problem behaviors are likely to occur, the procedures and data collection of FA are precise, and expertise in the visual analysis of graphs and data is needed to interpret data. Thus, functional analysis is typically not the assessment methodology of choice to complete an FBA in school settings.

Step 5: Form Hypothesis Statements

After you gather information, the final step of the FBA is to form hypotheses about the variables maintaining each challenging behavior. A hypothesis is simply an 'educated guess' about the environmental reasons for each behavior based on the assessment data you gathered in Step 2. Hypotheses can be stated in a narrative format or can be diagrammed according to the MOs, antecedents, and reinforcing consequences for each problem response.

Because MOs are often temporally distant from problem behaviors, you may not be able to pinpoint the MO for a particular response. This is reflected in the spaces with question marks under the MO variable. It is also important to note that some problem behaviors may have multiple MOs, antecedents, or maintaining consequences. In these cases, it is best to diagram each set of contingencies separately, as you see in the first two diagrams of Figure 7.5. The different consequences maintaining the same problem behaviors are in bold. In this example, it appears that yelling and cursing are maintained by both positive reinforcement in the form of attention and negative reinforcement in the form of escape. Therefore, any behavior intervention strategy should address both of these maintaining consequences.

Critically, the FBA and resulting hypothesis statements are not the final product of the process. The final product is a successful intervention plan that reduces the student's challenging behaviors. If the resulting behavior interventions are not successful, the team must reflect on the data gathered in the FBA and reconsider their hypotheses statements or, if necessary, collect additional data to pinpoint controlling variables. In essence, an FBA is useless if it does not lead to reducing the student's challenging behaviors.

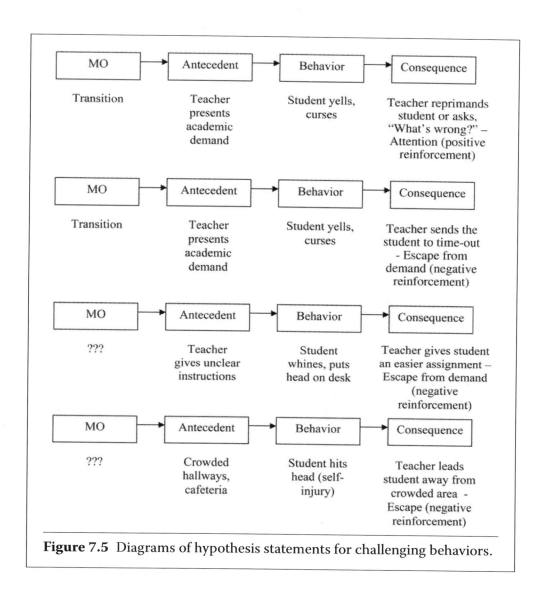

Figure 7.5 Diagrams of hypothesis statements for challenging behaviors.

The FBA Summary Report

The product of the FBA is a written report that summarizes information gained in each step of the process, concluding with hypothesis statement(s) for each challenging behavior. Figure 7.6 contains an example FBA report.

Functional behavioral assessment summary report: A written report that summarizes information gained in each step of the FBA process, concluding with hypothesis statements for challenging behaviors.

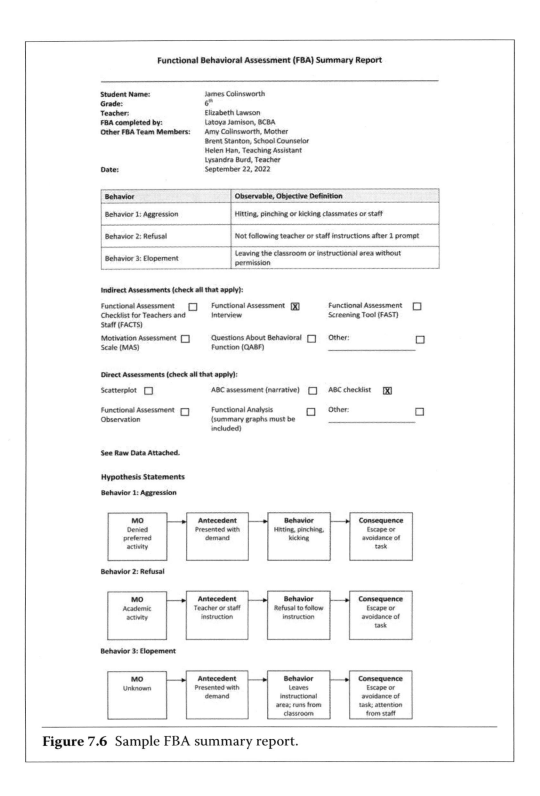

Figure 7.6 Sample FBA summary report.

As you consider whether an FBA is technically sound based on the FBA summary report, the following key questions bear consideration:

1. Are relevant team members who know the student and their behavior included on the FBA team?
2. Is team membership reflective of the student's culture and identity?
3. Is at least one expert in the FBA process, such as a BCBA, on the FBA team?
4. Does the report contain concise observable, objective definitions of all the relevant target behaviors?
5. Did the team use at least one indirect assessment and at least one direct assessment to determine behavior functions?
6. Do the hypothesis statements address all variables (i.e., MOs, antecedents, and consequences) controlling each behavior?
7. Does each variable represent a malleable, observable event in the student's environment? For example, presenting a work demand is an observable event in the student's environment within the teacher's control. Thus, presenting a work demand could be an MO or a trigger for the student's challenging behavior. In contrast, variables such as 'frustration' and 'anxiety' are not observable or malleable events in the student's environment, and thus they cannot be an MO or a trigger for challenging behavior.

Putting it Together: FBA and Behavior Intervention Programming

In this chapter, you have learned about the reasons why students engage in challenging behaviors. You have also discovered how to identify whether it is necessary to conduct the FBA, and how to convene the FBA team, define problem behaviors, gather information, and form hypotheses about environmental variables that support those behaviors. Once the FBA is completed, we must use this information to devise intervention strategies to eliminate the problem behavior, or at least reduce it to tolerable levels. In the next chapter, we will explore ways to develop interventions based on behavior functions. The decision-making process for conducting FBA and implementing BIP is depicted in Figure 7.7.

As we discussed, the initial step is determining whether it is necessary to conduct an FBA. If the behavior is severe (e.g., aggression, significant property destruction) and impedes the student's learning or learning of others, then we should immediately proceed to convene the FBA team and implement the remaining steps in the FBA/BIP process. An important consideration here is

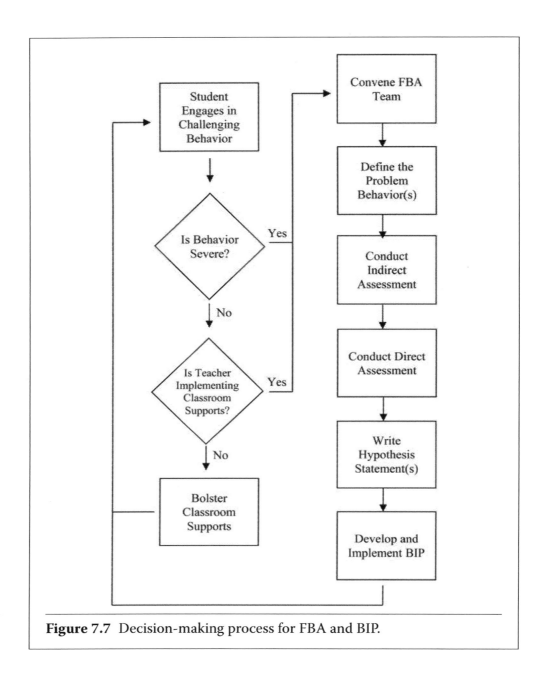

Figure 7.7 Decision-making process for FBA and BIP.

whether the student has an IEP and whether federal or state statutes, or school regulations, require the student to have an individualized BIP at this point. If the behavior is not severe, and there is no pressing legal or regulatory requirement to conduct an FBA, then we should assess whether the teacher is implementing sufficient classroom/secondary-level PBS strategies. If not, we should seek to bolster the teacher's implementation of the strategies and reassess whether the student is responsive to them and whether the behavior is reduced to manageable levels. If so, and the behavior is significant enough to warrant intervention, then we should convene the FBA team and implement the remaining steps in the FBA/BIP process. Importantly, following implementation of the BIP, we should reassess the student's responsiveness to our individualized strategies and then reimplement the decision-making process, if needed.

Summary

FBA is a collection of strategies to identify the environmental reasons why students engage in challenging behaviors for the purpose of developing effective interventions. The environmental reasons for challenging behaviors are MOs, which alter the momentary value of reinforcers and the frequency of behaviors associated with those reinforcers; antecedents or S^Ds, which trigger challenging behaviors; and reinforcing consequences, including positive and negative reinforcement. There are five steps in conducting an FBA. Step 1 is to determine whether an FBA is necessary. Step 2 is to convene the FBA team. Step 3 is to define the problem behaviors. Step 4 is to gather information through indirect and direct assessment. Step 5 is to form hypothesis statements about each problem behavior. FBA leads to the development of a function-based BIP to prevent and reduce problem behaviors.

Blank forms for the scatterplot, ABC assessment, ABC checklist, and FBA summary report are found in Figures 7.8, 7.9, 7.10, and 7.11 at the end of the chapter.

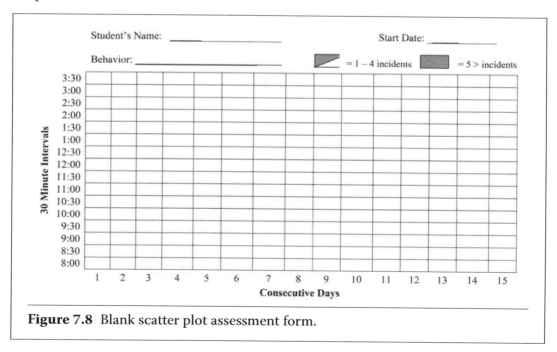

Figure 7.8 Blank scatter plot assessment form.

	Student:		Observer:		Date:

Time begin: **Time end:** 3:00

Time	Antecedent	Behavior	Consequence

Figure 7.9 Blank ABC assessment datasheet.

Student: _____				
Date/Time/Initial	Act/Location	Antecedent	Behavior	Consequence
Date: Time: Initial:	Activity: Location:	☐ Teacher delivered demand ☐ Teacher ended preferred activity ☐ Teacher delivered social attention ☐ Teacher attention diverted ☐ Peer within close proximity ☐ Requested assistance ☐ Engaged in leisure activity ☐ Alone, doing nothing ☐ Transitioning between locations ☐ Other: _____	☐ Aggression ☐ Out-of-seat ☐ Disruption ☐ Destroying ☐ Off-task ☐ Self-injury ☐ Disruption Define:_____ ☐ Out of seat ☐ Mouthing ☐ Other: _____	☐ Behavior ignored ☐ Redirected ☐ Reprimanded ☐ Provided with assistance ☐ Provided with item(s): _____ ☐ Escaped task ☐ Continued with task ☐ Other:_____
Date: Time: Initial:	Activity: Location:	☐ Teacher delivered demand ☐ Teacher ended preferred activity ☐ Teacher delivered social attention ☐ Teacher attention diverted ☐ Peer within close proximity ☐ Requested assistance ☐ Engaged in leisure activity ☐ Alone, doing nothing ☐ Transitioning between locations ☐ Other: _____	☐ Aggression ☐ Out-of-seat ☐ Disruption ☐ Destroying ☐ Off-task ☐ Self-injury ☐ Disruption Define:_____ ☐ Out of seat ☐ Mouthing ☐ Other: _____	☐ Behavior ignored ☐ Redirected ☐ Reprimanded ☐ Provided with assistance ☐ Provided with item(s): _____ ☐ Escaped task ☐ Continued with task ☐ Other:_____
Date: Time: Initial:	Activity: Location:	☐ Teacher delivered demand ☐ Teacher ended preferred activity ☐ Teacher delivered social attention ☐ Teacher attention diverted ☐ Peer within close proximity ☐ Requested assistance ☐ Engaged in leisure activity ☐ Alone, doing nothing ☐ Transitioning between locations ☐ Other: _____	☐ Aggression ☐ Out-of-seat ☐ Disruption ☐ Destroying ☐ Off-task ☐ Self-injury ☐ Disruption Define:_____ ☐ Out of seat ☐ Mouthing ☐ Other: _____	☐ Behavior ignored ☐ Redirected ☐ Reprimanded ☐ Provided with assistance ☐ Provided with item(s): _____ ☐ Escaped task ☐ Continued with task ☐ Other:_____

Figure 7.10 Blank ABC checklist form.

Functional Behavioral Assessment (FBA) Summary Report

Student Name:
Grade:
Teacher:
FBA completed by:
Other FBA Team Members:
Date:

Behavior	Observable, Objective Definition
Behavior 1:	
Behavior 2:	
Behavior 3:	
Behavior 4:	
Behavior 5:	

Indirect Assessments (check all that apply):

Functional Assessment Checklist for Teachers and Staff (FACTS) ☐   Functional Assessment Interview ☐   Functional Assessment Screening Tool (FAST) ☐

Motivation Assessment Scale (MAS) ☐   Questions About Behavioral Function (QABF) ☐   Other: ☐ _____

Direct Assessments (check all that apply):

Scatterplot ☐   ABC assessment (narrative) ☐   ABC checklist ☐

Functional Assessment Observation ☐   Functional Analysis (summary graphs must be included) ☐   Other: ☐ _____

See Raw Data Attached.

Figure 7.11 Blank FBA summary report.

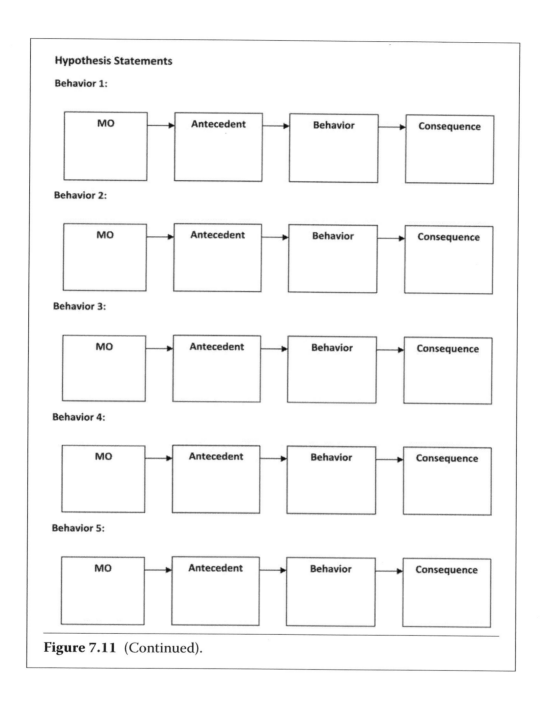

Figure 7.11 (Continued).

Key Terms

ABC assessment – A type of FBA direct assessment in which the observer records every instance of the challenging behavior, including the time the behavior occurred, what happened just before the behavior, and what happened just after the behavior.

ABC checklist – A variation of the ABC assessment with predefined antecedents, behaviors, and consequences.

Antecedents – Stimuli that trigger challenging behaviors, also known as discriminative stimuli (S^Ds).

Behavior intervention program (BIP) – A written plan, based on a functional behavioral assessment, that describes procedures to prevent and reduce a student's challenging behaviors.

Board-certified behavior analyst (BCBA) – A related-service provider with expertise in FBA and applied behavior analysis strategies.

Direct assessment – Observing the student in settings where problem behaviors occur and collecting data to discover patterns between antecedents, behaviors, and consequences.

Formal indirect assessments – Questionnaire and rating scales to systematically identify behavior functions.

Functional analysis – Experimental manipulation of variables thought to maintain challenging behaviors for the purpose of identifying behavior functions.

Functional behavioral assessment – A collection of strategies to identify the environmental reasons why students engage in challenging behaviors for the purpose of developing effective interventions. These include indirect assessments, direct assessments, and functional analysis.

Functional behavioral assessment summary report – A written report that summarizes information gained in each step of the FBA process, concluding with hypothesis statements for challenging behaviors.

Indirect assessment – Interviewing people who know the student to gather information about variables maintaining problem behaviors.

Motivating operations (MOs) – Events that alter the momentary value of reinforcers and the frequency of behaviors associated with those reinforcers.

Scatter plot – A type of FBA direct assessment that uses a grid to identify patterns in problem behaviors across time.

CHAPTER 8

Function-Based Interventions and Behavior Intervention Programming

Chapter Objectives

- Describe how multicomponent interventions and contextual fit are critical in behavior intervention programming.

- Identify interventions to address motivating operations.

- Understand interventions to change antecedents.

- Describe interventions to teach alternative behaviors.

- Explain strategies to modify reinforcing consequences.

- Understand how to implement and evaluate function-based behavior intervention programming.

DOI: 10.4324/9781003237228-8

In this chapter, you will learn how to use information gathered in the functional behavioral assessment (FBA) to develop function-based interventions and behavior intervention programming. First, we will discuss the importance of multicomponent interventions and contextual fit in reducing challenging behaviors. Then, we will explore interventions to address motivating operations, change antecedents or discriminative stimuli, teach alternative behaviors, and address consequences that reinforce problem behaviors. Finally, you will learn how these elements combine into a comprehensive behavior intervention program. We will overview how to train staff to implement the plan, and how to monitor the staff's procedural fidelity in implementing the plan.

PBS and Multicomponent Interventions

You will recall from Chapter 1 that PBS involves *multicomponent interventions*, which means that several strategies are simultaneously used to prevent and eliminate problem behaviors (Carr et al., 2002). Multicomponent interventions are more likely to be successful if a particular procedure does not work because others may 'fill the gap' to reduce targeted responses. Moreover, because the FBA is likely to identify more than one controlling variable, function-based behavior intervention programs (BIPs) should employ multiple strategies to address motivating operations, antecedents, reinforcing consequences, and teaching alternative responses.

In a review of positive behavioral intervention research targeting young children's challenging behaviors published between 1999 and 2008, O'Dell et al. (2011) noted that 48% of studies published in the *Journal of Positive Behavior Interventions* employed multicomponent interventions to successfully reduce problem behaviors. Multicomponent interventions have been used to reduce challenging behaviors of young children and adolescents with autism (Waters et al., 2009), traumatic brain injury (Gardner et al., 2003; Feeney, & Ylvisaker, 2003), and adults with intellectual disabilities (Cannella et al., 2006).

PBS and Contextual Fit

Contextual fit: Compatibility of the BIP with variables in the educational environment.

Contextual fit is another important component of successful BIPs. Contextual refers to the compatibility of the BIP with variables in the educational environment (Albin et al., 1996). These are (a) characteristics of the person for whom the plan is designed; (b) variables related to the people who will implement the plan; and (c) features of environments and systems within which the plan will be implemented (p. 82). BIPs that are designed with these features in mind are more likely to work because they will have greater coherence with the student, the people who implement the BIP, and the classroom, school, or other settings that the student occupies. Contextual fit is also a key component of culturally responsive PBS when plans are developed with voices that reflect the student's culture, and the culture of the larger school community.

The following guidelines will help you develop BIPs with good contextual fit (Tincani, 2007):

❏ *Seek team input.* Importantly, the BIP should be created with the input of those who will implement the plan, including teachers, teaching assistants, parents, and related services providers (e.g., speech-language pathologists). Recognize disagreement among the team and, when a particular member disagrees with one or more components, offer that member an alternative way to support the plan. Understand that everyone brings different expertise to the process. For instance, teachers and other professionals possess expert knowledge about specific behavior interventions, while parents know the student best, including their strengths and preferences. To ensure interventions are culturally responsive, we should actively seek the input of team members, including parents and extended family members, who reflect the student's culture and the culture of the larger community (Vincent et al., 2011).

❏ *Assess capacity of the team to support the BIP.* As the team selects intervention strategies, consider whether members will have the time, expertise, and necessary resources to implement the procedures with fidelity. Members may need to be trained on specific components, and some strategies may be precluded from the plan because they are resource intensive. In other cases, additional resources will need to be introduced to support interventions.

❏ *Assess compatibility of the BIP with school-wide programs and administrative supports.* There are many competing demands in the school setting, including the student's participation in high-stakes testing, placement in the general education classroom, and participation in school-wide academic and behavioral program initiatives. Consider how the BIP will be supported by, or will conflict with, competing initiatives and programs in the school. It may be beneficial for the team to create a prioritized list of interventions and implement those with higher priority first.

Next, we will discuss specific strategies to address motivating operations and antecedents, teach alternative behaviors, and change consequences that support problem behaviors.

Interventions to Address Motivating Operations

As you learned in Chapter 7, motivating operations (MOs) alter the momentary value of reinforcers and the frequency of behaviors associated with those reinforcers (Laraway et al., 2003). Common examples of MOs that increase the likelihood of challenging behaviors are difficulty with the morning routine, sleep deprivation, changes in staffing, or loss of a preferred activity (see Chapter 5). MOs are sometimes temporally distant from challenging behaviors; that is, they happen one or more hours before problem behaviors occur. This presents a challenge to intervention because you may not know that a particular MO has happened or you may not be able to alter the MO. For instance, as a teacher, there is probably little that you can do to change the student's sleep patterns in the home setting.

Next, we will discuss three strategies to address MOs, which involve communicating the MO across settings, removing the MO, and neutralizing the MO.

Communicate the MO Across Settings

Once you have identified an MO that increases the likelihood of challenging behaviors, it is important to communicate the presence of the MO across settings. For example, if disruption in the morning routine increases the likelihood of a student's difficult behaviors during the school day, the teacher may arrange for the parent to communicate about the event in a home-school communication notebook. Similarly, if a fight in another classroom is likely to increase a student's problem behaviors in your classroom, you should encourage teachers to communicate the occurrence of fights or other disruptive events prior to the student's arrival in your classroom. This way, you will be prepared to intervene when the MO happens.

Remove the MO

Perhaps the most obvious way to reduce the effects of an MO is to remove it (Horner et al., 1996); however, removing the MO is only practical under certain circumstances. For example, if an unpredictable schedule increases the reinforcing value of escape-maintained problem behaviors, the teacher can change the classroom routine to make it more predictable and structured, thus making the problem behavior irrelevant for the student. Unfortunately, under many circumstances, it will not be possible to eliminate the MO because it occurs in another setting (e.g., home, other classroom) or you do not have the ability to remove it (e.g., illness, loss of a preferred activity). In these cases, another alternative is to neutralize the MO.

Neutralize the MO

A *neutralizing routine* is a practical intervention to address the MO in many classroom circumstances. A neutralizing routine is an intervention to reduce the reinforcing value of a problem behavior when a MO has occurred (Iovannone et al., 2017; Horner et al., 1997; Sprague &

> **Neutralizing routine**: An intervention to reduce the reinforcing value of a problem behavior when a motivating operation has occurred.

Thomas, 1997). In effect, the neutralizing routine is another MO that 'cancels' the effects of the MO for a problem behavior. For example, if the student's loss of a preferred activity is an MO that increases the reinforcing value of challenging behaviors, we could offer the student an alternative preferred activity or give the student a choice of activities. If a traumatic event in the home setting increases the reinforcing value of difficult behaviors when the student is presented with a hard assignment, we could provide her with more assistance, make the assignment easier (e.g., fewer problems, easier problems), or provide precorrections about what she is supposed to do if she has a hard time (e.g., ask for help). Table 8.1 shows examples of MOs and neutralizing routines to counter those MOs.

Importantly, the neutralizing routine you choose will be specific to the student, the problem behavior, and the MO. Thus, the team's knowledge of the student and his preferences is critical in selecting the neutralizing routine. When a MO has occurred, be aware of specific antecedents that trigger problem behaviors. For instance, when a student has been denied a preferred activity, he may only engage in problem behaviors in the presence of a specific cue, such as when his errors are corrected (see, for example, Horner et al., 1997). In these cases, it is important to avoid delivering cues that will trigger challenging behaviors following the MO.

TABLE 8.1

Examples of motivating operations and neutralizing routines

Motivating operations	Neutralizing routines
Difficulty with the morning routine (e.g., getting up late, missing the bus) Argument before school Argument in another class	Allow student extended downtime or a preferred activity when s/he arrives in class; provide a more preferred assignment; provide more frequent breaks
Illness Sleep deprivation	Provide student with a nap if sleep deprived; allow for a choice of tasks; give more frequent breaks
Lack of attention from staff or peers Presence or absence of a specific staff person Presence or absence of a specific classmate	Give extra, non-contingent attention to the student; pair the student with an alternative, preferred staff person or student
Unpredictable schedule Disorganized transitions	Use precorrections to remind the student about upcoming events; implement an individual activity schedule; use pictures to cue the next activity
Loss of a preferred activity	Allow the student to engage in an alternative, preferred activity; provide a choice of activities

ACTIVITY

Identify a hypothetical MO for a student's problem behavior, and describe one strategy to neutralize the MO. Do not use one of the examples from the book.

_____

_____

_____

_____

_____

_____

_____

_____

_____

_____

_____

_____

_____

_____

_____

_____

_____

_____

_____

_____

_____

Interventions to Change Antecedents

The FBA is likely to identify one or more academic, social, or other environmental situations that trigger problem behaviors. Often, these antecedents can be modified to reduce or eliminate problem behaviors and promote student skills (Butler & Luiselli, 2007; Conroy & Stichter, 2003; Kern & Clemens, 2007; Luiselli et al., 2005; Stichter et al., 2009). We will explore four specific categories of antecedents and how they can be modified to prevent difficult behaviors. These involve the general environment and routine, social interaction, preferred activities, and non-preferred activities and demands. Table 8.2 shows specific antecedents and strategies to eliminate those antecedents as triggers for problem behaviors.

General Environment and Routine

Examples of possible triggers involving the general environment and routine include noisy classrooms, aversive sensory stimuli (e.g., sounds, lights), unplanned disruptions in the schedule, disorganized transitions, or unstructured routines. Interventions to address these antecedents include moving the student to a less noisy area of the room or providing an activity schedule to make the classroom routine more predictable.

Social Interaction

Social interaction triggers include the presence of a non-preferred person (or any person) in close proximity, crowded classrooms, or staff using particular words, phrasing, or tone of voice when interacting with the student, such as when providing instructions. Possible strategies to address social interaction antecedents include changing the student's proximity to others or changing the manner in which staff verbally interact with the student (e.g., saying 'I need you to start your work right now' versus saying 'It's time to begin your assignment, you have 15 minutes and then you can take a break.')

TABLE 8.2

Examples of triggering antecedents and interventions

Triggering antecedents	Interventions
General environment and routine ❑ Noisy classroom ❑ Aversive sensory stimuli (e.g., sounds, lights) ❑ Unplanned schedule disruption ❑ Disorganized transition ❑ Unstructured schedule	Move student to a quieter location. Move student away from aversive sensory stimuli; remove stimuli. Use precorrections to signal unplanned changes in routine; offer an alternative, preferred activities. Add signals to cue transitions; make transitions brief. Use individual and class-wide activity schedules. Increase consistency in the classroom schedule. Increase active student responding.
Social interaction ❑ Close proximity to others ❑ Close proximity to non-preferred persons ❑ Crowded classroom ❑ Verbal interactions (voice tone, wording)	Move the student away from others. Pair or group the student with preferred persons. Pair non-preferred persons with preferred activities. Change wording of instructions and other verbal interactions. Maintain a positive tone with student during verbal interactions. Make verbal interactions concrete and direct (e.g., 'What are you doing?' versus 'Please begin your assignment.'
Preferred items and activities ❑ Toys, games, instructional materials	Provide an array of preferred items and activities. Provided choices when preferred items and activities are not available. Provide a choice of preferred instructional materials.
Non-preferred activities and demands ❑ Academic and other non-preferred assignments ❑ Non-preferred routines	Provide a choice of assignments. Include student interests in assignments. Add preferred stimuli to assignments and routines (e.g., materials, people). Decrease the difficulty of assignments. Decrease work requirements. Make assignments more challenging. Provide more frequent breaks. Alternate demanding and preferred activities.

Preferred Items and Activities

The presence of preferred items and activities can also evoke challenging behaviors. For instance, if another child has a toy that our student wants, he might hit the child to obtain the toy. Interventions to address preferred items and activities as triggers include providing the student with a choice of preferred items, having an array of items available, and teaching the student to make an alternative selection when a particular item is not available.

Non-Preferred Activities and Demands

Finally, non-preferred activities and demands such as chores or academic assignments can trigger challenging behaviors. In these cases, we can modify the activity or demand in some way to make it less aversive, offer a choice of activities, or remove the demand. For instance, we could reduce the number of problems the student must complete before taking a break, allow the student to choose a partner to work with on the assignment, or offer an alternate assignment.

ACTIVITY

Identify a hypothetical antecedent for a student's problem behavior related to the general environment and routine, social interaction, preferred items and activities, or non-preferred activities and demands. Describe a way that you could change the antecedent so that it does not trigger the student's problem behavior. Do not use one of the examples from the book.

_____

_____

_____

_____

_____

_____

_____

_____

_____

_____

_____

_____

_____

_____

_____

_____

_____

_____

_____

Teaching Alternative Behaviors

Functional communication training (FCT): Teaching the student an alternative, appropriate response that produces the same reinforcing consequences as the problem behavior.

In addition to modifying MOs and antecedents, it is essential to teach alternative behaviors. *Functional communication training* (FCT) involves teaching the student an alternative, appropriate response that produces the same reinforcing consequences as the problem behavior. FCT makes problem behaviors irrelevant by teaching the student a better way to produce desired consequences (Carr & Durand, 1985; Dunlap et al., 2006; Durand & Merges, 2001; Ghaemmaghami et al., 2021).

It is important to understand that FCT isn't simply teaching the child better communication skills. Rather, FCT is a specific, two-step process. First, FBA data are collected to identify antecedents and consequences reinforcing the challenging behavior. Once we identify these, an alternative behavior that produces the same consequences is taught in situations where the problem behavior is likely to occur. So, FCT strategies *must* be based on results from an FBA. For example, in their seminal study on FCT, Carr and Durand conducted an FBA and found that children's problem behaviors were more likely in conditions involving low levels of adult attention and high levels of task difficulty. In these situations, children's behaviors were reinforced by attention from adults. They reduced challenging behaviors by teaching children to request adults' attention during low attention conditions, or to request an adult's assistance when a difficult task was presented.

The diagrams in Figure 8.1 illustrate contingencies maintaining two problem behaviors, hitting and screaming (bottom), and appropriate, alternative behaviors that produce the same consequences, asking for help and asking for a break (top).

You should use the following guidelines when you teach alternative responses through FCT (Durand & Merges, 2001).

❏ Ensure that the alternative response you teach will produce the same reinforcing consequences as the problem behavior(s).
❏ Chose a response modality that others are likely to recognize and reinforce. For example, a voice output communication device may not be a good choice in a noisy classroom, or if staff will not always be in close

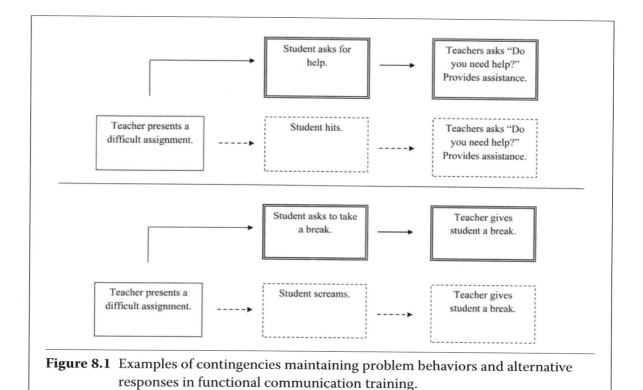

Figure 8.1 Examples of contingencies maintaining problem behaviors and alternative responses in functional communication training.

proximity to the student. In these circumstances, it might be best to teach the student a highly recognizable response, such as hand-raising.

❏ Teach an alternative response that will be easier for the student to perform than the problem behavior. In general, it is best to teach a response modality that the student already knows. For instance, if the student primarily communicates by exchanging pictures, then picture exchange is probably the modality of choice.

❏ Provide a high level of reinforcement for the alternative response. For FCT to be successful, the alternative response must be more efficient at producing reinforcing consequences than the problem behavior. Initially, you should prompt the alternative response frequently and heavily reinforce it. As the student learns the response independently, you can thin the schedule of reinforcement to one that is reasonable for most classroom situations.

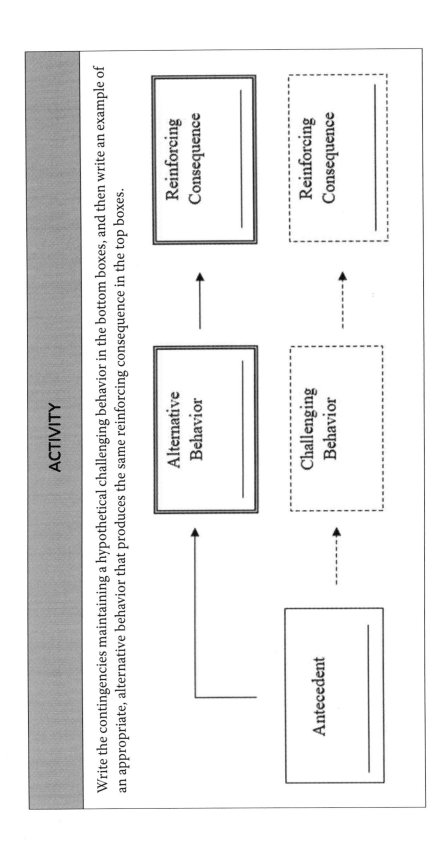

ACTIVITY

Write the contingencies maintaining a hypothetical challenging behavior in the bottom boxes, and then write an example of an appropriate, alternative behavior that produces the same reinforcing consequence in the top boxes.

Reinforcing Consequence

Reinforcing Consequence

Alternative Behavior

Challenging Behavior

Antecedent

Interventions to Address Consequences

There are two categories of consequence-based interventions to reduce challenging behaviors: removing consequences for problem responses and adding consequences to support alternative responses. We will explore each.

Removing Reinforcing Consequences for Problem Responses

In Chapter 7, you learned that extinction happens when you stop delivering a reinforcer for a behavior, and consequently, the student performs the behavior less frequently. Thus, a basic strategy to reduce problem responses is to stop delivering consequences that reinforce them. For example, if a student engages in aggressive behavior to obtain adult attention, then you should stop delivering attention when she behaves aggressively.

However, extinction is never recommended as a stand-alone procedure to reduce problem behaviors for the following reasons. First, extinction often accompanies a phenomenon called extinction burst, that is, when you stop delivering the reinforcer, the frequency and/or intensity of the behavior initially increases before it decreases. When extinction burst occurs, it can be very difficult to withhold the reinforcer as rates of the problem behavior increase. For example, when ignored, a student may begin screaming so loudly that classroom instruction cannot continue. Second, extinction does not teach any alternative responses, thus the student is likely to resume engaging in problem behaviors in situations where the reinforcer cannot be withheld. Therefore, it is always best to combine extinction with other intervention procedures, including FCT, as part of a multicomponent BIP (Fisher et al., 1993; Shukla & Albin, 1996; Waters et al., 2009).

Consider the following guidelines to remove consequences for problem behaviors maintained by attention, escape, and access to preferred items.

> *Attention-maintained problem behaviors.* Avoid making eye contact with or talking to the student following the problem behavior. Prompt the student to engage in an alternative response using the least intrusive prompt possible; gestural prompts are optimal. If you must respond to problem behaviors, remain calm, keep a neutral tone of voice, and minimize your physical interactions with the student.
>
> *Escape-maintained problem behaviors.* Prompt the student to continue the activity using the least intrusive prompt (e.g., gestures); if the student is younger or has a severe intellectual disability, it may be necessary to

physically block the student from escaping; if so, follow your school's or agency's procedures for physical engagement of students and only use as much physical effort as is necessary to keep the student in the activity. Provide prompts for the student to engage in alternative responses. Provide a high level of reinforcement if the student has engaged in the alternative response in the absence of problem behaviors.

Item-access-maintained problem behaviors. Block the student's access to the preferred item; minimize your verbal or physical interactions with the student. Prompt the student to engage in an alternative response (e.g., asking for the item, picking an alternative item). Provide a high level of reinforcement for alternative responses in the absence of problem behaviors.

Add Reinforcing Consequences for Appropriate Responses

As you place problem behaviors on extinction, teach alternative responses, address MOs, and change antecedents, it is critical that you add reinforcing consequences for appropriate behaviors. The basic rule is to provide behavior-specific praise, tokens, and other types of reinforcement (see Chapter 6) when the student engages in appropriate behaviors, and to minimize reinforcement for problem behaviors. Remember, if you are conducting FCT, it is critically important to provide a high level of reinforcement for alternative responses at first, and then to thin the schedule of reinforcement to one that is appropriate for the classroom or other school situations.

Differential reinforcement of other behavior (DRO): Providing reinforcement to the student if they refrained from engaging in problem behaviors for a pre-specified period of time.

Differential reinforcement of other behavior (DRO) is another reinforcement-based procedure to reduce challenging behaviors. DRO involves providing reinforcement to the student after he has refrained from engaging in one or more problem behaviors for a pre-specified period of time (Cooper et al., 2020; Poling & Ryan, 1982). For example, in a DRO-15, if the student refrains from engaging in challenging behaviors for 15-minutes, she will earn a reinforcer at the end of the 15-minute interval. However, if she engages in the challenging behavior at any time during the 15-minutes, she loses the opportunity to earn the reinforcer. The DRO interval can then be reset, and the student can have another opportunity to earn the reinforcer if they refrain from the behavior for 15-minutes. Presumably, the 'other behavior' in DRO is anything the student is doing while not performing problem behaviors. While DRO can be effective, a major drawback is that a student needn't be doing anything to earn the reinforcer; she simply needs to refrain from problem behaviors. Therefore, like extinction, DRO should only be used in combination with other function-based intervention strategies, including FCT, which you have learned about in this chapter.

The following are steps for implementing DRO:

- ❏ Identify the target behavior.
- ❏ Identify the reinforcer the student will earn for the DRO. If the student's FBA showed a specific consequence reinforcing their challenging behavior (e.g., peer attention, escape from demands), that consequence should be incorporated into the DRO reinforcer. For example, if the student's problem behavior is maintained by peer attention, the student could earn time playing games with peers as their DRO reinforcer. Alternatively, if the student's problem behavior is reinforced by the escape from demands, they could earn an extra break from work as their DRO reinforcer. In other cases, the student could be given a choice of reinforcers from a menu.
- ❏ Determine the DRO interval. Typically, this is done by taking a baseline measurement of the problem behavior's frequency during a specific time period, and then dividing the frequency of the behavior by the time period. For example, if three instances of hitting are observed during a 60-minute period, and three divided by 60 is 20, then the initial DRO interval would be 20 minutes (DRO-20).
- ❏ Use a timer to signal the beginning of the DRO interval.
- ❏ If the student refrains from the target behavior during the entire interval, immediately provide the reinforcer.
- ❏ If the student engages in the problem behavior during the interval, you may reset the timer and allow the student another opportunity to earn the reinforcer.
- ❏ If the student is repeatedly successful in earning the reinforcer, incrementally increase the DRO interval. For example, if the student is consistently able to refrain from the problem behavior for 20 minutes, the DRO interval could be increased to 25 minutes, 30 minutes, and so on.

A different reinforcement-based procedure for reducing challenging behaviors is *differential reinforcement of low rates of behavior* (DRL). In DRL, the student

Differential reinforcement of low rates of behavior (DRL): Providing reinforcement to the student if they perform a problem behavior less than a pre-specified number of times within a pre-specified period of time.

earns a reinforcer if they perform the behavior less than a pre-specified number of times within a pre-specified time period (Cooper et al., 2020; Dietz & Repp, 1973). For example, if we implement a DRL-5 during a 45-minute reading class, the student will earn the reinforcer at the end of the 45-minute class if they performed the behavior five or fewer times. If they performed the behavior more than five times during the 45-minute class, they would lose the opportunity to earn the reinforcer at the end of 45-minutes.

DRL can be a good alternative to DRO under the following conditions: 1) the student performs the behavior at a very high rate and therefore it is unlikely we can eliminate the behavior altogether; and/or 2) it is acceptable for the student to perform the behavior at low levels. For instance, we might decide DRL is an acceptable procedure for a student who exhibits high frequencies of calling-out during class, but not an acceptable procedure for a student who hits their peers during class.

The following are steps for implementing DRL:

- ❑ Identify the target behavior.
- ❑ Identify the reinforcer the student will earn for the DRL. As with DRO, the reinforcer should be the same reinforcer for challenging behavior identified in the FBA. Or a choice of reinforcers should be provided.
- ❑ Determine the DRL criterion and the DRL interval. This is done by taking a baseline measurement of the behavior during a specified time period. The DRL criterion should be set lower than the baseline level of behavior during that time period. For example, if the student engaged in 15 instances of calling-out during a 45-minute class, we could establish a DRL-5, where the student earns a reinforcer if they call out five or fewer times during the 45 minutes.
- ❑ If the student meets the DRL criterion, immediately provide the reinforcer.
- ❑ If the student does not meet the DRL criterion, you can reset the DRL interval and allow the student another opportunity to earn the reinforcer.
- ❑ If the student is consistently successful in meeting the DRL criterion in earning their reinforcer, consider decreasing the DRL criterion, or transitioning to a DRO.

Putting It Together: Developing a Comprehensive Behavior Intervention Program

You have now learned how to collect data on why problem behaviors are occurring through FBA, and how to use this information to develop a function-based

BIP. Figure 8.2 reviews the steps of this process. In Figure 8.3, you will find a form that can be used to develop the written BIP.

The top of the form contains the same information about the student and the BIP team as found in the FBA summary report. In addition, there is a space to write a review date for the team to reevaluate the plan. Section I of the form contains spaces to write observable definitions of up to five target behaviors. Each behavior should have a name (e.g., hitting) along with an observable

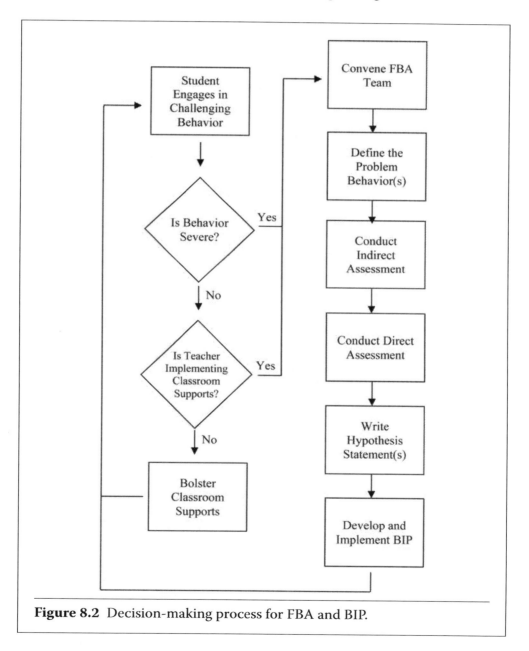

Figure 8.2 Decision-making process for FBA and BIP.

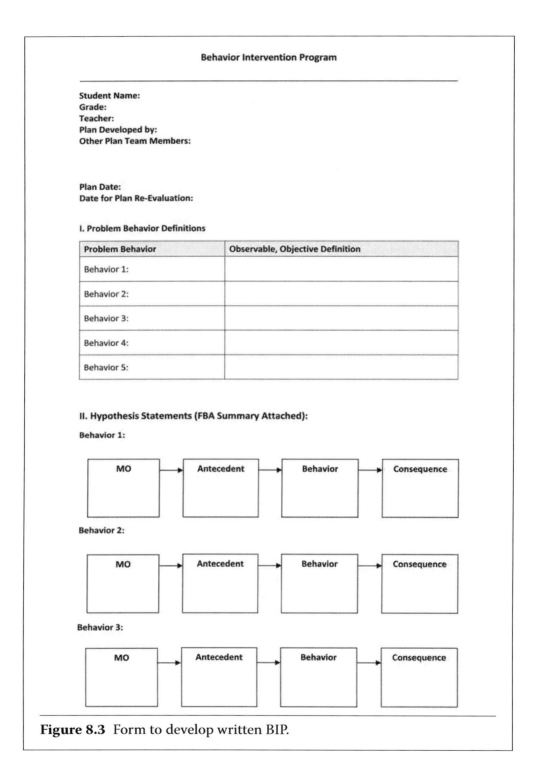

Figure 8.3 Form to develop written BIP.

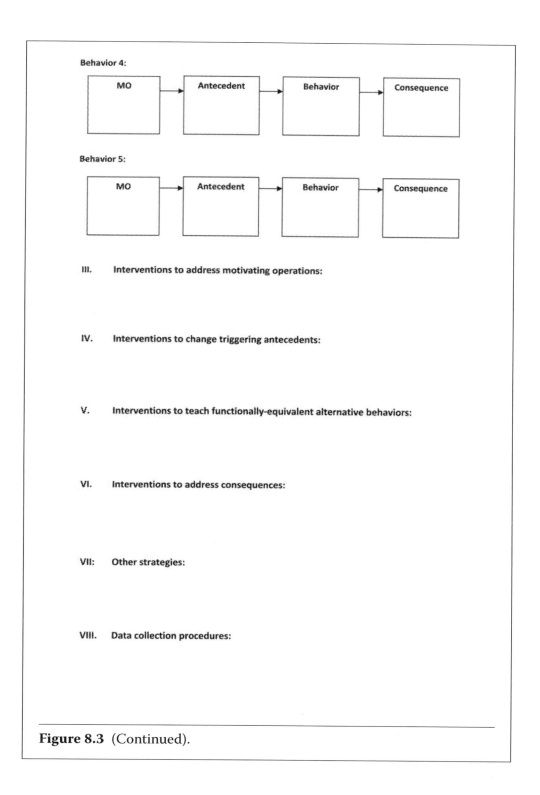

Behavior 4:

| MO | → | Antecedent | → | Behavior | → | Consequence |

Behavior 5:

| MO | → | Antecedent | → | Behavior | → | Consequence |

III.   Interventions to address motivating operations:

IV.   Interventions to change triggering antecedents:

V.   Interventions to teach functionally-equivalent alternative behaviors:

VI.   Interventions to address consequences:

VII: Other strategies:

VIII.   Data collection procedures:

Figure 8.3 (Continued).

definition (e.g., forcefully striking another person with a hand or foot). Section II contains diagrams to write the MOs, antecedents, and consequences maintaining each problem behavior. This information is gathered from the FBA. If a particular variable is not known, then 'unknown' can be written in the space below the variable. Sections III, IV, V, and VI contain spaces to describe interventions to address MOs, modify triggering antecedents, teach alternative behaviors, and address reinforcing consequences. Importantly, the procedures should be written clearly so that anyone implementing the plan can understand the plan and execute it with fidelity. Section VII includes a space to write other BIP procedures. These could include crisis management procedures or special instructions for the plan.

An important part of implementation is monitoring the BIP to ensure that it is working. Data should be collected on each target response (see Chapter 9). Data can be collected on the frequency of target behaviors (i.e., how many times the behavior happens per period or day), rate of target behaviors (i.e., how many times the behavior happens per minute or per hour), or the duration of target behaviors (i.e., how long does the target behavior occur) before and after intervention. Data should be reviewed at least weekly to determine if the plan is reducing target behaviors, and the team should convene at least bi-weekly to determine whether the plan needs to be changed. Section VIII of the BIP permits the team to outline data collection procedures for the plan.

Figure 8.4 contains an example BIP, based on the example FBA provided in Chapter 7 (see Figure 7.6). Note how the procedures in sections III, IV, V, and VI correspond with the functions of behavior identified in the FBA. The plan also includes procedures for responding to the student's aggression in section VII and an overview of data collection procedures in section VIII.

Implementing, Monitoring, and Evaluating the BIP

Initial training on the BIP. Once you have developed the BIP, the next step is to implement it. The first step of implementing the plan is to train all staff who will be responsible for carrying out the procedures outlined. As we learned in Chapter 2, *behavioral skills training* (BST) is an empirically supported strategy to teach skills, including instructions, modeling of the skills, opportunities for practice, and performance-based feedback (Kirkpatrick et al., 2019; Sarokoff & Sturmey, 2004). BST utilizes the same principles of behavior and teaching strategies you have learned about in this book. We can use BST as a framework to teach staff to implement the plan with the following steps:

❏ *Provide the written BIP to all staff responsible for implementation.* Ask staff to carefully review the plan and write down any questions they

Behavior Intervention Program

Student Name:	James Colinsworth
Grade:	6th
Teacher:	Elizabeth Lawson
Plan Developed by:	Latoya Jamison, BCBA
Other Plan Team Members:	Amy Colinsworth, Mother Brent Stanton, School Counselor Helen Han, Teaching Assistant Lysandra Burd, Teacher
Plan Date:	October 3, 2022
Plan Re-Evaluation Date:	November 7, 2022

I. Problem Behavior Definitions

Problem Behavior	Observable, Objective Definition
Behavior 1: Aggression	Hitting, pinching or kicking classmates or staff
Behavior 2: Refusal	Not following teacher or staff instructions after 1 prompt
Behavior 3: Elopement	Leaving the classroom or instructional area without permission

II. Hypothesis Statements (FBA Summary Attached):

Behavior 1: Aggression

Behavior 2: Refusal

Behavior 3: Elopement

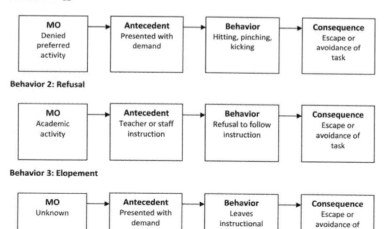

III.   Interventions to address motivating operations:

Aggression: When James is denied a scheduled preferred activity, staff should immediately offer an alternative preferred activity. They should remind James when he will next be able to access the denied activity.

Figure 8.4 Sample BIP.

Refusal: When possible, James should be allowed to choose the order in which he complete class activities. When this is not possible, James should be allowed to select a partner to wo with, or an area of the classroom where he is allowed to work.

IV.   Interventions to change triggering antecedents:

Aggression and Elopement: When James is presented with a demand, such as a written assignment, staff should periodically remind him about following the classroom rules. Staff should also periodically remind him about his check-in / check-out system and the reward he is earing for following classroom / rules and completing assignments.

Refusal: When giving instructions to James, staff should pause and ask James if he has any questions before he begins an assignment. Staff should remind James if he has any questions or problems to use his assistance card to ask for assistance (see below). Staff should also remind James that he can ask for a break (see below).

V.   Interventions to teach functionally-equivalent alternative behaviors:

Aggression, Refusal, and Elopement: At the beginning of the day, James will be provided with five break cards and five help cards that he may use throughout the day. At the beginning of the day, the cards should be placed on his desk. If needed, staff should remind James about his opportunities to use the cards. At any time, James may hand a break card to a staff person to earn a brief five-minute break from work. At the conclusion of the break, James must immediately return to his instructional area and continue working. At any time, James may also hand a help card to staff, who should immediately provide assistance to James in his instructional area. Use of the help card does not constitute a break, and James should continue working on his assigned work after staff has provided assistance.

VI.   Interventions to address consequences:

Aggression, Refusal, and Elopement: James will participate in the classroom check-in / check-out system, where he earns a reward each day in exchange for points he accrues for following classroom rules and completing his work in the absence of challenging behaviors. Staff should also provide frequent behavior-specific praise to James, with a ratio of 4:1 praise to behavior correction statements.

VII: Other strategies

Aggression: When James is aggressive towards peers or staff, he should be immediately verbally redirected and physically redirected , if necessary, to maintain safety or himself, staff, and students. Staff should follow the school's crisis response de-escalation procedures, if necessary.

VIII.   Data collection procedures:

Aggression: Frequency count data will be collected on aggression during all periods.

Refusal: Frequency count data will be collected on refusal during all periods.

Elopement: Frequency count data will be collected on refusal during all periods.

All data will be graphed and reviewed by the BCBA, Latoya Jamison, at least weekly.

Figure 8.4 (Continued).

have. Provide at least one day for review. After they have read the plan and formulated questions, give them an opportunity to ask their questions and provide clarification, as necessary.

❏ *Review the written plan.* Review all procedures in the written plan face-to-face and explain them to staff. Clarify the rationale for each of the strategies in relation to the problem behaviors and results of the FBA. Any technical procedures (e.g., functional communication training, check-in/check-out, token systems) will require explanation for staff who have never implemented them before. Give staff an opportunity to ask questions.

❏ *Model the procedures.* Demonstrate how to perform each of the behavior support procedures in the plan. For example, if the plan includes behavior-specific praise, you might set up a role play where one staff person pretends to be a student who engages in appropriate behaviors. When the 'student' is being good, demonstrate how you would apply behavior-specific praise. Similarly, if the plan includes FCT, show how you would prompt and reinforce the student for performing the desired alternative response. Give staff another opportunity to ask questions.

❏ *Provide opportunities for practice with feedback.* Ask staff to demonstrate the procedures outlined in the plan, which you have modeled. For instance, you could break staff into dyads and ask them to take turns being the student and staff perform who applies the procedures. Importantly, you should actively monitor staff as they practice and provide positive and corrective feedback. Give staff another opportunity to ask clarifying questions.

It is critical to make the BIP available for everyone on the team who will be responsible for executing the program. Therefore, the BIP should be readily available in the classroom or included on a clipboard with the student's data sheets or other instructional materials.

Ensuring Procedural Fidelity

Procedural fidelity (also called *treatment integrity*) is the extent to which procedures in the written BIP are implemented as described (Gresham, 1989). Procedural fidelity is vitally important to the student

> **Procedural fidelity**: The extent to which procedures in the written BIP are implemented as described.

and their BIP. High procedural fidelity increases the likelihood of successful outcomes for the student; however, low procedural fidelity prevents the plan from working as intended by the team. Procedural fidelity can be lower than optimal for any number of reasons. If the BIP is ineffective because it is not function-based, staff are more likely to abandon it and be more skeptical of similar intervention efforts in the future. If the plan has a low contextual fit because it was not developed with team input, is not culturally relevant, and/ or staff disagree with the procedures, they are also likely to abandon it. Similarly, if staff lack the training and resources to implement the plan properly, procedural fidelity may be low, or staff may stop implementing the plan altogether.

Conversely, the PBS strategies outlined in the book are designed to promote high procedural fidelity when we design plans that are function-based, have good contextual fit, are culturally responsive, and employ empirically supported interventions. If we employ BST to provide solid training for teachers and staff prior to implementing the plan, this will increase the likelihood of high procedural fidelity. Nonetheless, low procedural fidelity can occur for reasons beyond our control. For example, staff turnover may result in personnel with inadequate training implementing the BSP, increases in staff caseloads, or student-teacher ratios may render high fidelity implementation more challenging given competing demands.

The most common way to ensure high procedural fidelity once the plan is implemented is to monitor BIP implementation directly and provide feedback to staff on their implementation (Brady et al., 2019). Ideally, procedural fidelity monitoring and feedback should begin immediately after plan implementation and continue periodically throughout the implementation process. Often, a procedural fidelity evaluation is triggered when the student has a spike in challenging behavior, and the team has concerns about whether the spike in behavior is the result of low procedural fidelity. However, procedural fidelity monitoring should occur regularly regardless of whether the student is encountering significant behavioral difficulties. Usually, the expert point person on the BIP, such as a BCBA, is in the best position to conduct procedural fidelity monitoring.

The form in Figure 8.5 can be used to observe and monitor procedural fidelity directly. At the top of the form, there is space to write information about the observer, the student, the time and date of the observation, and the staff observed. In the table below, the left column contains spaces for the observer to write each of the function-based behavior interventions, other procedures, and data collection. The right column contains spaces for the observer to mark whether the procedure was fully implemented, partially implemented, or not at all implemented. If there was no occasion to observe the procedure (e.g., no task demands were presented), then the observer would mark 'not applicable.' At the bottom of the form, there is space for the observer to summarize the feedback they delivered to staff immediately following observation, any staff comments, and any action steps based on the observation. Figure 8.6 contains

Procedural Fidelity Monitoring Form

Observer: _____   Date: _____   Time: _____

Student: _____

Staff observed: _____

Procedure	Implemented?
Motivating Operation (MO) intervention(s):	Yes ___ No___ Partial ___ Not applicable ___ Comments:
Antecedent Interventions(s):	Yes ___ No___ Partial ___ Not applicable ___ Comments:
Alternative Behavior Intervention(s):	Yes ___ No___ Partial ___ Not applicable ___ Comments:
Consequence Intervention(s):	Yes ___ No___ Partial ___ Not applicable ___ Comments:
Other Intervention(s):	Yes ___ No___ Partial ___ Not applicable ___ Comments:
Data collection:	Yes ___ No___ Partial ___ Not applicable ___ Comments:

Feedback Delivered to Staff:

Staff Comments:

Action Steps:

Figure 8.5 Procedural fidelity monitoring form.

Procedural Fidelity Monitoring Form

Observer: __Latoya Jamison, BCBA__   Date: __10/17__   Time: __8:30 – 9:15 am__

Student: __James Colinsworth__

Staff observed: __Lasandra Burd, Helen Han__

Procedure	Implemented?
Motivating Operation (MO) intervention(s): Offer alternative preferred activity Offer choice of activities	Yes _X_ No___ Partial ___ Not applicable ___ Comments: James was offered a choice of activities
Antecedent Interventions(s): Reminders about classroom rules and check-in /check-out Reminders about asking for assistance and breaks	Yes ___ No___ Partial _X_ Not applicable ___ Comments: James was reminded to ask for assistance and breaks, but not about classroom rules or check-in check / check-out
Alternative Behavior Intervention(s): Help cards and break cards	Yes ___ No___ Partial _X_ Not applicable ___ Comments: Break cards were on the desk, but help cards were not. James requested a break once during the observation.
Consequence Intervention(s): Check – in / Check-out Behavior-specific praise	Yes _X_ No___ Partial ___ Not applicable ___ Comments: Ms. Han completed James' check-in / check out at the end of the period. Staff provided high rates of behavior specific praise.
Other Intervention(s): Crisis management for aggression.	Yes ___ No___ Partial ___ Not applicable _X_ Comments: No aggression observed.
Data collection: Frequency counts for aggression, refusal, and elopement	Yes _X_ No___ Partial ___ Not applicable ___ Comments: Data collection forms were present and being filled out for the day.

Feedback Delivered to Staff: I provided positive feedback to staff on their successful implementation of the procedures. I reminded them about the importance of giving James pre-corrections about following the classroom rules and his check-in / check-out system. I asked why James did not have access to his help cards.

Staff Comments: Staff thanked me for the observation and positive feedback. They stated that James has been doing very well with his academic work (math) and does not need to use his help cards.

Action Steps: Reconvene the team on 11/7 and revise the plan as needed based on staff feedback and progress data.

Figure 8.6 Example of a completed procedural fidelity monitoring form.

an example completed observation form based on the BIP example from earlier in this chapter.

What If the Plan Is Not Working?

Often, the team's BIP may not be effective in reducing target behaviors to acceptable levels or zero levels. BIPs can be unsuccessful for two critical reasons. First, information gathered in the FBA did not accurately identify variables maintaining the student's problem behaviors. Therefore, if the plan is not working the team should revisit the FBA and collect additional data to verify the functions of problem behaviors, and alternative hypotheses should be considered. Second, the plan may not be working because of low procedural fidelity. If so, the team should reconvene to discuss the program and consider ways to improve implementation. Often, this involves adding procedures, omitting procedures, or adjusting procedures to meet the preferences of team members or demands of the classroom or other school environments.

Summary

Function-based behavior intervention programs reduce challenging behaviors through modifying the environment according to information gathered in the functional behavioral assessment. BIPs include multicomponent interventions and should be developed with contextual fit, including input of the educational team and assessment of the team's capacity to support the program. The BIP contains interventions to address motivating operations, change triggering antecedents, teach alternative behaviors, and modify reinforcing consequences. This information is summarized in a written program. Staff should be trained to implement the plan using behavioral skills training, and procedural fidelity checks should be conducted to ensure the plan is being implemented as written. Data from the BIP should be reviewed at least weekly to determine effectiveness. If the plan is not working, the team should consider collecting additional FBA data and revising initial hypotheses and should verify that the program is being implemented with high fidelity.

Key Terms

Behavior intervention program (BIP) – A written plan that describes procedures to prevent and reduce a student's challenging behaviors.

Contextual fit – Compatibility of the BIP with variables in the educational environment.

Differential reinforcement of other behavior (DRO) – Providing reinforcement to the student if they refrained from engaging in problem behaviors for a pre-specified period of time.

Differential reinforcement of low rates of behavior (DRL) – Providing reinforcement to the student if they perform a problem behavior less than a pre-specified number of times within a pre-specified period of time.

Functional communication training (FCT) – Teaching the student an alternative, appropriate response that produces the same reinforcing consequences as the problem behavior.

Multicomponent interventions – Simultaneously applying several interventions to prevent and eliminate problem behaviors.

Neutralizing routine – An intervention to reduce the reinforcing value of a problem behavior when a motivating operation (MO) has occurred.

Procedural fidelity – The extent to which procedures in the written BIP are implemented as described.

CHAPTER 9

Using Data to Evaluate PBS Outcomes

Chapter Objectives

- Describe why data are critical to PBS outcomes.

- Given a target behavior, know how to select an appropriate data collection strategy and collect data.

- Describe the rationale and logic of A-B designs to evaluate PBS outcomes.

- Understand the basic components of line graphs and how to use line graphs to evaluate data.

DOI: 10.4324/9781003237228-9

This chapter describes the role of data in evaluating PBS outcomes. The importance of data in PBS will be discussed, followed by an overview of data collection strategies. Then, we will learn about the role of A-B designs in program evaluation and outline the differences between baseline and intervention conditions. Finally, we will summarize the basic components of line graphs and learn how to construct graphs for program assessment.

Why Are Data Important?

Data: Objective information about a behavior that enables a teacher to make informed decisions about PBS programming.

Data-based decision making: The ongoing process of using data to determine how well the student is doing and make program changes accordingly.

Suppose that you have implemented PBS strategies to reduce a student's challenging behaviors and increase their appropriate behaviors. How will you know that the program is working? A commonly employed strategy to evaluate behavior interventions is an informal one. You might think about differences between the student's behaviors before and after the intervention, or ask someone else, 'How are they doing since we started the program?' Your estimation of how well the student is doing will be influenced by your history with them, the opportunities you have to observe them (or lack thereof), and your opinions about their skills and the severity of their challenging behaviors. In other words, the resulting information will be subjective. Therefore, because informal evaluation is unlikely to yield accurate and reliable information about the student's progress, it is not a useful strategy to evaluate PBS programming.

A better approach involves the systematic use of data to assess program outcomes. *Data* are objective information about a behavior that enables a teacher to make informed decisions about PBS programming. *Data-based decision making* is the ongoing process of using data to determine how well the student is doing academically and behaviorally and make program changes accordingly (Wilcox et al., 2021). Importantly, the data we collect have no value unless we actively use them to evaluate and change the student's program according to their progress.

Accountability is another important reason to collect data. For example, for children with disabilities, the individualized education program (IEP) team will convene at least annually to review the students' progress in attaining special education program goals and objectives. Data provide a systematic means to evaluate IEP outcomes and hold team members accountable for their respective roles. Conversely, the absence of data may lead to questions about students' progress and the overall quality and appropriateness of special education programs.

Collecting Data

The data collection strategy you choose will be determined by the key characteristics of your student's target behaviors. We will focus on six strategies: event recording; rate recording; duration recording; latency recording; interval recording; and momentary time sampling. An overview of the five data collection strategies, characteristics of behaviors that are appropriate for each strategy, and examples of behaviors that are appropriate for each strategy are presented in Figure 9.1.

Strategy	Procedure	Appropriate for	Examples
Event recording	Record each time the student performs a behavior	Discrete behaviors; Behaviors that leave a permanent product which can be counted	Hand raising Hitting Writing numbers
Rate recording	Record each time the students performs a behavior, divide frequency of behavior by unit of time	Behaviors for which speed + accuracy is important; Observation periods which are variable in duration	Typing on a keyboard Orally reading Assembling packages
Duration recording	Record the amount of time the student engages in a behavior	Behaviors where time is an important dimension; Behaviors that have a definite beginning and end	Silently reading Playing with peers Crying
Latency recording	Record the time period between an instructional cue and when the student performs a behavior	Situations in which the student takes a long time to respond to a cue or instructions	Responding to teacher directions Leaving the building after a fire alarm Exiting the classroom after the bell
Interval recording	Dividing an observation period into equal intervals, and then recording whether the behavior has occurred during each interval	Behaviors that do not have a definite beginning or end; High rate behaviors; Multiple behaviors or multiple students	Self-stimulatory behavior On-task behavior Disruptive behavior
Momentary time sampling	Dividing an observation period into equal intervals, and then recording whether the behavior is occurring at the end of each interval	Same as interval recording	Same as interval recording

Figure 9.1 Overview of data collection strategies.

Event Recording

Event recording: Tallying each time the student performs a behavior, and then adding the tally marks to yield a frequency of the behavior per class period, session, or day.

Event recording involves recording each time the student performs a behavior, and then adding the tally marks to yield a frequency of the behavior per class period, session, or day. For example, Campbell and Lutzker (1993) used event recording to measure the impact of functional communication training (see Chapter 7) on throwing and destroying items, screaming, and sign language use of Don, a boy with autism. Event recording is most appropriate for behaviors that are discrete – that is, they have a definite beginning and end – and do not occur at such a high frequency that it is practically impossible to count them. For instance, event recording would not be appropriate for a student who engages in self-stimulatory rocking hundreds of times during the class period. Event recording is also not an appropriate strategy for behaviors that occur for longer time periods (e.g., silent reading); for these behaviors, duration recording is most appropriate (see below). Event recording is a useful strategy for behaviors that leave a permanent product that can be counted. For instance, spelling words correctly written on a worksheet or envelopes correctly labeled can be tallied to yield a frequency count.

Figure 9.2 shows a sample event recording data sheet for a student, James. The two rows contain hypothetical data for two behaviors, talking-out and hand-raising. The observer, Ms. Watkins, has tallied the frequency of each behavior during one-hour observation periods throughout the day. At the end

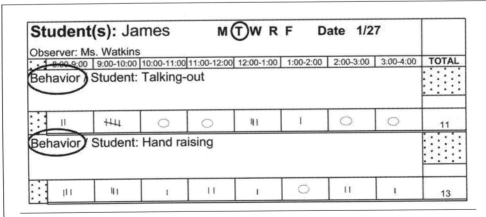

Figure 9.2 Sample event recording data sheet.

Student(s):   M   T   W   R   F   Date:

Observer:

								TOTAL
Behavior / Student:								
Behavior / Student:								
Behavior / Student:								
Behavior / Student:								
Behavior / Student:								
Behavior / Student:								
Behavior / Student:								

Figure 9.3 Blank event recording data sheet.

of the day, she adds the tally marks to determine the total frequency of the target behaviors.

The same form can be used to event record the behaviors of multiple students. In each row labeled 'Behavior/Student,' you can write the name of a student and the student's behavior that you are recording (e.g., teasing – Colin). Then, you can make tally marks for each student's behavior in the spaces below. A blank event recording form is found in Figure 9.3.

Rate Recording

Rate recording: A variation of event recording in which the total frequency of a behavior is divided by a unit of time (e.g., minutes, hours).

Rate recording is a variation of event recording that is appropriate when you are concerned with how quickly and accurately the student performs a behavior. Rate recording is also appropriate when the duration of your observation periods is variable. Like event recording, rate recording involves tallying each time the student performs a behavior and then adding the tally marks to yield a frequency of the behavior per class period, session, or day. However, with rate recording, you then divide the total frequency of a behavior by a unit of time (e.g., minutes, hours).

For certain behaviors, such as reading orally, writing answers to multiplication facts, or typing on a keyboard, you will be concerned with how quickly, as well as how accurately, the student performs the behavior. For instance, you might want a student to orally read 100 words per minute, write correct answers to 20 multiplication facts per minute, or type 120 words per minute. Rate recording is appropriate for such behaviors. The formula for calculating the rate of behavior is:

Frequency of behavior / time = rate

For example:

42 answers correct / 2 minutes = 21 answers correct per minute

Rate recording is also useful when you are collecting data on the frequency of a behavior, as in event recording, but the duration of your observation periods is variable. Consider the hypothetical data below:

Day	Monday	Tuesday	Wednesday	Thursday	Friday
Observation period	1 hour	1.5 hours	2 hours	1 hour	1.5 hours
Frequency	27	29	36	22	32
Rate per hour	27	19.3	18	22	21.3

If we look at the third row, which represents the frequency of behaviors, the behavior occurred at its highest frequency on Wednesday, 36, and at its lowest frequency on Thursday, 22. However, the duration of the observation periods – that is, the amount of time the student had an opportunity to perform the behavior – skews our frequency counts; shorter observation periods yield lower frequencies, while longer observation periods yield higher frequencies. For a more accurate measure of the behavior, we should convert the frequency to rate. Looking at the fourth row, rate per hour, we can see that the behavior occurred at its highest rate on Monday, 27, and at its lowest rate on Wednesday, 18. When observation periods are variable, it is necessary to convert frequency data to rate to yield the most accurate picture of the behavior.

Duration Recording

There are certain behaviors for which time is the most important dimension. Consider a student who has lengthy tantrums lasting up to 45 minutes. Event recording will probably not yield an accu-

> **Duration recording:** Recording the amount of time the student engages in a behavior.

rate picture of these behaviors, particularly if tantrums occur only once or twice per day. Instead, we should use *duration recording*, in which we record the amount of time the student engages in a behavior. Crozier and Tincani (2007) used duration recording to determine if Social Stories™ increased the amount of time that Thomas, a preschool student, sat during circle time. Other behaviors appropriate for duration recording include time spent working on homework, crying, or time out-of-seat.

Duration recording is only appropriate if you can determine when a behavior starts and stops. To conduct duration recording, the observer carries a stopwatch, smartphone, or another device equipped with a stopwatch application. When the behavior begins, the stopwatch is started; when the behavior stops, the stopwatch is paused. Data can be collected on the total duration of the behavior during an observation period, or the total duration can be divided by the frequency of the behavior to yield an average duration of the behavior per observation period.

Figure 9.4 contains a sample duration data recording sheet. Ms. Alvarez has recorded the duration of two behaviors, out-of-seat and tantrums. In each space under the cells labeled, 'Obs.,' she records the start and stop time for each behavioral episode. Then, in the space labeled, 'Total,' she writes the total duration of all of the behaviors during the observation. Finally, in the space labeled 'Average,' she writes the average duration of all of the behaviors, which is determined by dividing the frequency of behaviors by the total duration. Figure 9.5 contains a blank data sheet that can be used for duration recording.

Student (s): ___Rayna___   M T W (TH) F   Date: __4 / 28__

Observer: ___Ms. Alvarez___

Behavior /Student: Out-of-seat

Obs. 1	Obs. 2	Obs. 3	Obs. 4	Obs. 5	Obs. 6	Obs. 7	Obs. 8	Total	Average
:00 /:42	:43 / 1:28	1:29 / 2:36	2:37 / 3:01	3:02 / 3:31	3:32 / 4:02	4:03 / 4:47	4:48 / 5:02	5:02	38 s.

Behavior / Student: Tantrum

Obs. 1	Obs. 2	Obs. 3	Obs. 4	Obs. 5	Obs. 6	Obs. 7	Obs. 8	Total	Average
:00 / 5:24	5:25 / 10:17	10:18/ 15:21	__ / __	__ / __	__ / __	__ / __	__ / __	15:21	5 m. 12 s.

Figure 9.4 Sample duration data recording sheet.

Latency Recording

Latency recording: Recording the time period between an instructional cue and when the student performs a behavior.

Like duration recording, *latency recording* involves time as a unit of measurement. However, in latency recording, we measure the time period between an instructional cue and when the student performs a behavior. Latency recording is often used when we wish to reduce the amount of time it takes for a student to begin a task or comply with instructions. For example, Heinicke et al. (2009) used latency recording to evaluate the effects of rules and a token economy on reducing the amount of time it took for Claire, an adolescent girl with acquired brain injury, to comply with academic instructions. Other behaviors where latency recording is useful include time to transition from one activity to another or time required to exit the school building following an alarm during a fire drill.

Student (s): _____   M T W TH F   Date: _____

Observer: _____

Behavior / Student:									
Obs. 1	Obs. 2	Obs. 3	Obs. 4	Obs. 5	Obs. 6	Obs. 7	Obs. 8	Total	Average
___/___	___/___	___/___	___/___	___/___	___/___	___/___	___/___		

Behavior / Student:									
Obs. 1	Obs. 2	Obs. 3	Obs. 4	Obs. 5	Obs. 6	Obs. 7	Obs. 8	Total	Average
___/___	___/___	___/___	___/___	___/___	___/___	___/___	___/___		

Behavior / Student:									
Obs. 1	Obs. 2	Obs. 3	Obs. 4	Obs. 5	Obs. 6	Obs. 7	Obs. 8	Total	Average
___/___	___/___	___/___	___/___	___/___	___/___	___/___	___/___		

Behavior / Student:									
Obs. 1	Obs. 2	Obs. 3	Obs. 4	Obs. 5	Obs. 6	Obs. 7	Obs. 8	Total	Average
___/___	___/___	___/___	___/___	___/___	___/___	___/___	___/___		

Behavior / Student:									
Obs. 1	Obs. 2	Obs. 3	Obs. 4	Obs. 5	Obs. 6	Obs. 7	Obs. 8	Total	Average
___/___	___/___	___/___	___/___	___/___	___/___	___/___	___/___		

Behavior / Student:									
Obs. 1	Obs. 2	Obs. 3	Obs. 4	Obs. 5	Obs. 6	Obs. 7	Obs. 8	Total	Average
___/___	___/___	___/___	___/___	___/___	___/___	___/___	___/___		

Behavior / Student:									
Obs. 1	Obs. 2	Obs. 3	Obs. 4	Obs. 5	Obs. 6	Obs. 7	Obs. 8	Total	Average
___/___	___/___	___/___	___/___	___/___	___/___	___/___	___/___		

Behavior / Student:									
Obs. 1	Obs. 2	Obs. 3	Obs. 4	Obs. 5	Obs. 6	Obs. 7	Obs. 8	Total	Average
___/___	___/___	___/___	___/___	___/___	___/___	___/___	___/___		

Figure 9.5 Blank duration data recording sheet.

ACTIVITY

Below are a set of hypothetical data representing the number of words orally read per minute. In the row labeled rate per minute, calculate the rate of behavior for each day by dividing the frequency of behavior by unit of time (minutes). Space is provided below for your calculations, if needed.

Day	Monday	Tuesday	Wednesday	Thursday	Friday
Observation period	2 minutes	4 minutes	3 minutes	4 minutes	2 minutes
Frequency	220	484	290	442	248
Rate per minute					

The data sheet shown in Figure 9.5 can also be used for latency recording as well. Instead of recording the duration of each behavior, the teacher would start the stopwatch when an instructional cue is given, and then stop the stopwatch when the student performs the behavior. As with duration recording, the latencies can be summed and then divided by the number of behaviors to yield an average latency for each observation period.

Interval Recording

Our next data collection strategy, *interval recording*, involves dividing an observation period into equal intervals and then recording whether the behavior occurs during each interval. There are two variations of interval recording. In *partial-interval recording*, we record if the behavior occurs during *any part* of the interval; in *whole-interval recording*, we record if the behavior occurs during the *entire* interval.

Interval recording is the preferred data collection strategy under three conditions. First, if it is difficult for observers to tell when the behavior starts and stops, interval recording is useful because it does not require the observer to note the beginning or end of behaviors. Interval recording is also a good strategy for very high-rate behaviors that cannot be tallied with event or rate recording. Finally, interval recording is useful when recording multiple behaviors or the behaviors of multiple students. Although interval recording is advantageous in these situations, a substantial limitation of interval recording versus event, rate, duration, and latency recording is that it provides only an indirect measure of the

Interval recording: Dividing an observation period into equal intervals and then recording whether the behavior occurs during each interval.

Partial-interval recording: A type of interval recording in which the behavior is recorded if it occurs during any part of the interval.

Whole-interval recording: A type of interval recording in which the behavior is recorded if it occurs during the entire interval.

behavior. Therefore, interval recording should only be used with behaviors for which the other recording systems are inappropriate.

The two variations of interval recording, partial-interval recording and whole-interval recording, are prescribed under different circumstances. Partial-interval recording tends to overestimate the occurrence of a behavior, and therefore is used to measure challenging behaviors that we want to reduce. For example, Haley et al. (2010) used partial-interval recording to measure the effects of antecedent cue cards on reducing the vocal stereotypy (e.g., repetitive sounds, humming) of Sean, an eight-year-old boy with autism.

Whole-interval recording, in contrast, tends to underestimate the occurrence of behavior, and is often used when we are trying to measure academic, social, communicative, or other behaviors that we want to increase. Graham-Day et al. (2010) collected data with whole-interval recording to assess the effects of self-monitoring and reinforcement on the on-task behaviors of three tenth-grade students with attention deficit hyperactivity disorder (ADHD).

Figure 9.6 shows a hypothetical interval recording data sheet for Madison. Mr. Chen is measuring Madison's rocking and repetitive vocalizations using partial-interval recording. The observation period, which lasts for five minutes, has been divided into 30-second intervals. Mr. Chen makes a plus mark if the behavior occurs during any part of the interval; he makes a zero mark if the behavior does not occur during any part of the interval. The resulting data can be converted to a percentage of intervals; therefore, Madison engaged in rocking for 40% of intervals and repetitive vocalizations for 30% of intervals during the five-minute observation period. Figure 9.7 has a blank form that can be used for partial or whole-interval recording.

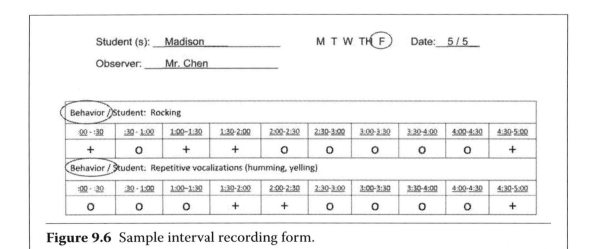

Figure 9.6 Sample interval recording form.

Student (s): _____   M T W TH F   Date:_____

Observer: _____

Behavior / Student:									

Behavior / Student:									

Behavior / Student:									

Behavior / Student:									

Behavior / Student:									

Behavior / Student:									

Behavior / Student:									

Behavior / Student:									

Figure 9.7 Blank interval recording form.

Momentary time sampling:
Dividing an observation period into equal intervals, and then recording whether the behavior is occurring at the end of each interval.

Interval recording is a useful strategy when you are attempting to record several behaviors simultaneously or the behaviors of several students simultaneously. Figure 9.8 shows a partial-interval recording data sheet for three students to measure three behaviors – hitting, screaming, and asking. The data sheet represents a rotating observation system; the observer records the behavior of Student 1 during the first interval, Student 2 during the second interval, Student 3 during the third interval, and so on. The rotating observation system results in fewer intervals of data; however, it enables the scorer to capture data on more behaviors than would be possible with a continuous recording system.

Our final data collection strategy, *momentary time sampling*, is like interval recording in that we divide our observation period into equal intervals. However, the observer records only whether the behavior is occurring at the *end* of each interval (i.e., at the moment each interval is ending). Typically, the end of the interval is cued by a repeating signal (e.g., beep from a timer) that tells the observer when to record. The primary advantage of momentary time sampling is that it does not require the recorder to continually observe behaviors. This is a significant practical advantage in classroom situations where the teacher must simultaneously deliver instruction and collect data. Momentary time sampling also enables the observer to collect data on several students and several behaviors at the same time.

Student (s): _____ M T W TH F Date:_____

Observer: _____

| A = Asking | S = Screaming |
| H = Hitting | |

Interval	Time	Student 1	Student 2	Student 3
1	:10	(H) S A	H S A	H S A
2	:20	H S A	H S (A)	H S A
3	:30	H S A	H S A	(H) (S) A
4	:40	H S (A)	H S A	H S A
5	:50	H S A	(H) S A	H S A
6	1:00	H S A	H S A	H (S) (A)
7	1:10	H S (A)	H S A	H S A
8	1:20	H S A	H S A	H S A
9	1:30	H S A	H S A	H (S) A
10	1:40	H S A	H S A	H S A
11	1:50	H S A	H S (A)	H S A
12	2:00	H S A	H S A	H (S) A
13	2:10	H (S) A	H S A	H S A
14	2:20	H S A	H (S) A	H S A
15	2:30	H S A	H S A	H (S) A
16	2:40	H (S) A	H S A	H S A
17	2:50	H S A	(H) (S) A	H S A
18	3:00	H S A	H S A	H S (A)
19	3:10	H (S) A	H S A	H S A
20	3:20	H S A	H S (A)	H S A
21	3:30	H S A	H S A	H (S) A
22	3:40	H (S) (A)	H S A	H S A
23	3:50	H S A	H S A	H S A
24	4:00	H S A	H S A	H S (A)
25	4:10	H (S) A	H S A	H S A
26	4:20	H S A	H S (A)	H (S) A
27	4:30	H S A	H S A	H S A
28	4:40	H S A	H S A	H S A
29	4:50	H S A	(H) S A	H S A

Figure 9.8 Sample partial-interval recording data sheet for three students to measure three behaviors.

ACTIVITY

In the space below, describe a student's hypothetical academic, social, or challenging behavior that you wish to measure. Identify which of the six data collection systems is most appropriate to measure the behavior and why. Discuss any practical constraints that affected your selection of the data collection system.

_____

_____

_____

_____

_____

_____

_____

_____

_____

_____

_____

_____

_____

_____

_____

_____

_____

_____

_____

A disadvantage of momentary time sampling is that it provides the least direct measure of behaviors and tends to overestimate or underestimate behaviors. Inaccuracies are more likely with longer intervals (i.e., one minute or greater; Rapp et al., 2008). The data sheet in Figure 9.7 can also be used for momentary time sampling.

A-B Designs to Evaluate PBS Outcomes

Once you have selected a data collection system, your next step is to collect and graph your data. Remember, the primary reason for collecting data is to evaluate PBS programming and make any needed changes to the intervention. Therefore, you want to collect data frequently to provide an accurate picture of the student's progress. For some behaviors, you

A-B design: A single-subject design that compares a person's behavior under a baseline condition with no intervention (A) to a second condition, in which an intervention is applied (B).

should collect data on a daily basis; for others, collecting data two to three times per week or once per week will be sufficient. Data should be reviewed at least weekly to assess students' progress with PBS programming.

A-B designs provide a means to evaluate the relationship between a behavior and your intervention. A-B designs is a type of single-subject design that compares a person's behavior under a baseline condition with no intervention (A) to a second condition, in which an intervention is applied (B). A-B designs employ baseline logic (Tincani & Travers, 2018), which is illustrated by Figure 9.9.

The top panel of Figure 9.9 shows a graph for hitting with five baseline data points (left). The dotted lines show the range of the data points. If the teacher continued to collect data for additional days, do you think the behavior would improve? It would probably not. The dotted lines on the right side of the graph indicate that the behavior would likely continue at its baseline level if no intervention was applied.

In contrast, the bottom panel shows a graph in which an intervention was applied to reduce hitting. Visual inspection of the graph shows that the behavior was reduced below its baseline level during the intervention; therefore, we can conclude that the intervention was successful in reducing the student's hitting below its baseline level.

How long should you collect baseline data before implementing your intervention? Typically, a minimum of three to five data points are necessary; however, as illustrated in Figure 9.9, your baseline data should be stable enough (or

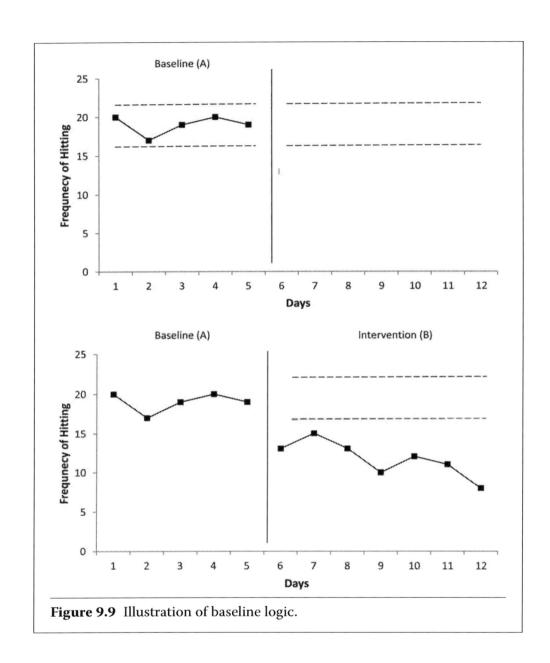

Figure 9.9 Illustration of baseline logic.

trending in a worsening direction) for you to predict that the behavior would not improve without intervention.

Graphing Data

Five essential components should be included on every behavior graph. The graph in Figure 9.10 shows the effects of an intervention involving functional communication training, precorrections, and a token economy on the duration of a student's tantrums. The critical elements are:

a. *Y-axis.* Shows the behavior's level and has a descriptive label that describes the behavior and how it was measured (e.g., total duration of hitting).
b. *X-axis.* Depicts the passage of time and shows the unit measurement (e.g., school days, class periods, hourly sessions).
c. *Data path.* Data points represent the level of behavior for each observation period with lines to connect the data points.
d. *Condition labels.* Describes the condition that was in effect during data collection. Interventions are briefly described

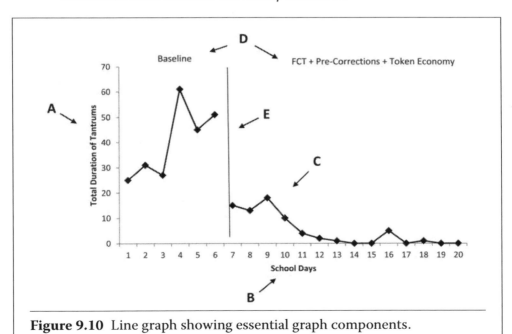

Figure 9.10 Line graph showing essential graph components.

e. *Condition change line.* Indicates the change of one condition (e.g., baseline) to another (e.g., intervention). The data points on either side of the condition line are not connected.

Importantly, you should graph your data frequently to assess your student's progress with the program. It is best to graph your data points daily or as often as you collect data.

What if the program is not working? Your graph may show that the student's behavior remains at baseline level after you implement the intervention. As we learned in Chapter 8, interventions can fail for a number of reasons, including the failure of interventions to address the functions of challenging behaviors and lack of procedural fidelity. In some cases, it will be necessary to change interventions or add interventions in order to reduce problem behaviors to acceptable levels.

Figure 9.11 shows a graph depicting the effects of two interventions on the percentage of intervals of disruption. The first intervention, response cards, failed to reduce disruption below its baseline level. Therefore, the teacher had to add a second intervention – or C condition – the good behavior game, which reduced disruption to acceptable levels.

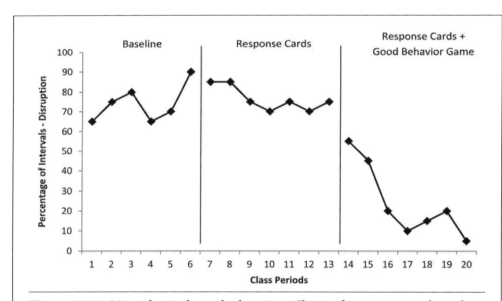

Figure 9.11 Hypothetical graph showing effects of response cards and response cards plus the good behavior game on classroom disruption.

Summary

Data are necessary to evaluate PBS programming and to hold team members accountable for their respective roles. Your data collection system – event, rate, duration, latency, interval recording, or momentary time sampling – should be selected according to key characteristics of the behavior(s) you wish to measure. Data on target behaviors should be collected frequently and evaluated on at least a weekly basis. A-B designs permit you to compare your student's performance before and after intervention. Graphs contain essential information about a student's performance and allow you to visually assess his or her progress and make program changes accordingly.

ACTIVITY

In the space below, draw a line graph showing the effects of an intervention on a hypothetical student's challenging behavior. The graph should show baseline and intervention conditions and should contain the five essential elements described earlier – the Y-axis, X-axis, condition, data path, condition labels, and condition change line(s).

Key Terms

A-B Design – A single-subject design that compares a person's behavior under a baseline condition with no intervention (A) to a second condition, in which an intervention is applied (B).

Data – Objective information about a behavior that enables a teacher to make informed decisions about PBS programming.

Data-based decision making – The ongoing process of using data to determine how well the student is doing and make program changes accordingly.

Duration Recording – recording the amount of time the student engages in a behavior.

Event recording – Tallying each time the student performs a behavior, and then adding the tally marks to yield a frequency of the behavior per class period, session, or day.

Interval recording – Dividing an observation period into equal intervals and then recording whether the behavior occurs during each interval.

Latency recording – Recording the time period between an instructional cue and when the student performs a behavior.

Momentary time sampling – Dividing an observation period into equal intervals, and then recording whether the behavior is occurring at the end of each interval.

Partial-interval recording – A type of interval recording in which the behavior is recorded if it occurs during any part of the interval.

Rate recording – A variation of event recording in which the total frequency of a behavior is divided by a unit of time (e.g., minutes, hours).

Whole-interval recording – A type of interval recording in which the behavior is recorded if it occurs during the entire interval.

CHAPTER 10

Putting It Together

Evidence-Based Classroom Management Inventory

The Evidence-Based Classroom Management Inventory (EB-CMI) is a tool to assess teachers' implementation of classroom management and PBS strategies. This chapter overviews how to implement and score the EB-CMI and use the results to improve your classroom management and PBS practices.

In this book, you have learned about many strategies for reducing your students' challenging behaviors and increasing their appropriate behaviors through positive behavior support. The EB-CMI below summarizes key areas of classroom management and provides a means for you to evaluate and improve your performance in these areas. If you are currently teaching, complete the survey to develop an action plan for improving your classroom management skills. If you are not currently teaching, once you have your own classroom you can complete the survey to reflect on your future classroom management skills and identify key areas for improvement. If you are a related services provider, consultant, or administrator, you can use the EB-CMI to evaluate, support, and provide feedback to teachers in their classroom management practices.

The survey is divided into two sections. Part I allows you to evaluate your performance for each classroom management skill we have covered in the book. Part II enables you to select the classroom management area for which you need the most improvement and to develop an action plan to increase your skill in one to three specific skills. Repeat the survey as often as needed to reflect on your classroom management performance.

DOI: 10.4324/9781003237228-10

Reflective Classroom Manager Survey

Teacher's Name:_____

Date:_____

Grade/Subject:_____

School:_____

Instructions

Part I: For the key components of classroom management below, circle 1–5 to indicate the extent to which each is in place in the classroom:

- ❏ 1 = totally not in place,
- ❏ 2 = mostly not in place,
- ❏ 3 = partially in place,
- ❏ 4 = mostly in place
- ❏ 5 = totally in place, or
- ❏ n/a = not applicable.

For some areas, you may indicate n/a if they do not apply to your classroom. For example, if you do not have any students with significant challenging behavior, then you would circle n/a for the items pertaining to functional behavior assessment (FBA) and behavior intervention plans (BIPs). *Circle n/a only if there is a specific reason the practice does not apply; do not circle n/a simply because you feel the area should not be a priority*. Determine the average score for each classroom management area by adding the total score and dividing by the total possible score, as shown in the boxes.

    Part II: For the classroom management areas with the *lowest average scores*, select one to three key components for improvement. For example, if Classroom-Wide Behavior Support receives your lowest score, you might select contingent praise and attention, classroom rules, or active supervision for improvement. Then, in the following spaces, describe your action plan for improving your performance on the three components (e.g., I will seek student input to create a set of classroom rules, post them, and develop a lesson plan for teaching them). Then, identify a time for your achieving and evaluating your improvement plan.

    Revisit the survey as often as necessary to reflect on your classroom management performance and to target key areas for improvement.

Part I

	In place?
Culturally responsive PBS (Chapter 3)	
❑ Lessons reflect an awareness of students' cultures	1 2 3 4 5 n/a
❑ Lessons are designed to allow active participation of all students in the class	1 2 3 4 5 n/a
❑ Voices of diverse students, their families, and the community are incorporated in academic and behavioral strategies	1 2 3 4 5 n/a
❑ Data are used to evaluate for disproportionality in discipline practices; strategies are in place for reducing disproportionality, if needed	1 2 3 4 5 n/a
Comments:	
Classroom organization (Chapter 4)	
Student schedules (pp. 48–57)	
❑ Demanding and preferred activities are alternated	1 2 3 4 5 n/a
❑ Long activities are broken up into shorter activities, as appropriate	1 2 3 4 5 n/a
❑ Choices are offered	1 2 3 4 5 n/a
❑ Whole class schedule is posted	1 2 3 4 5 n/a
❑ Individual student schedules are in place, as appropriate	1 2 3 4 5 n/a
Comments:	
Physical space (pp. 58–60)	
❑ Classroom is neat	1 2 3 4 5 n/a
❑ Instructional areas are clearly defined	1 2 3 4 5 n/a
❑ Seating is arranged according to activities and students' needs	1 2 3 4 5 n/a
❑ Seating is arranged to minimize student distractions	1 2 3 4 5 n/a
❑ Physical space is arranged to accommodate students with limited mobility	1 2 3 4 5 n/a
Comments:	

Transitions (p. 61)	
❏ Activity transitions are brief	1 2 3 4 5 n/a
❏ End of activities is signaled by a clear cue	1 2 3 4 5 n/a
❏ All lesson preparation is completed before lessons begin	1 2 3 4 5 n/a
Working with teaching assistants (pp. 61–62)	1 2 3 4 5 n/a
❏ Performance expectations are explicit	1 2 3 4 5 n/a
❏ Ongoing feedback is provided	1 2 3 4 5 n/a
Comments:	
Classroom organization average	__ / __ = __
Active student responding (Chapter 5)	
❏ Response cards are used to promote ASR (pp. 67–71)	1 2 3 4 5 n/a
❏ Choral responding is used to promote ASR (p. 71)	1 2 3 4 5 n/a
❏ Guided notes are used to promote ASR (pp. 72–73)	1 2 3 4 5 n/a
❏ Other strategies (e.g., technology) are used to promote ASD	1 2 3 4 5 n/a
Brisk instructional pacing is used (pp. 76–77)	
❏ Lessons are organized	1 2 3 4 5 n/a
❏ Wait-time is minimized, as appropriate	1 2 3 4 5 n/a
❏ Intertrial intervals are minimized	1 2 3 4 5 n/a
❏ Feedback is immediately provided	1 2 3 4 5 n/a
Comments:	
Active student responding average	__ / __ = __
Classroom-wide behavior support (Chapter 6)	1 2 3 4 5 n/a
❏ Contingent praise and attention is delivered at a 4:1 ratio (pp. 90–92)	1 2 3 4 5 n/a
❏ Behavior-specific praise is delivered (pp. 92–93)	1 2 3 4 5 n/a
❏ Students are taught to appropriately recruit teacher attention (pp. 94–96)	1 2 3 4 5 n/a
❏ Errors are systematically corrected (p. 97)	1 2 3 4 5 n/a
❏ Classroom rules are posted and rule following is reinforced (pp. 97–100)	1 2 3 4 5 n/a

❏ Group contingencies are in place (pp. 101–106)	1 2 3 4 5 n/a
❏ Active supervision is occurring (p. 106)	1 2 3 4 5 n/a
Comments:	
Classroom-wide behavior support average	__ / __ = __
FBA and function-based interventions (Chapters 7–8)	
❏ Functional behavioral assessments are conducted for students with chronic challenging behaviors	1 2 3 4 5 n/a
❏ Function-based behavior intervention plans are implemented for students with chronic challenging behaviors	1 2 3 4 5 n/a
Comments:	
FBA and function-based interventions average	__ / __ = __
Data collection (Chapter 9)	
❏ Data on challenging and appropriate behaviors are collected on an ongoing basis	1 2 3 4 5 n/a
❏ Data are converted in graphs and reviewed on at least a weekly basis	1 2 3 4 5 n/a
❏ Data are used to make changes to student programming	1 2 3 4 5 n/a
Comments:	
Data collection average	__ / __ = __

Part II

1. Classroom management area with lowest average score: _____
2. One to three key areas for improvement:

    a. _____

    b. _____

    c. _____

3. Action plan for improvement:

_____

_____

_____

_____

_____

_____

_____

4. I will complete and evaluate my action plan by (exact date):

_____

_____

_____

_____

_____

_____

_____

Glossary

- **A-B Design**: A single-subject design that compares a person's behavior under a baseline condition with no intervention (A) to a second condition, in which an intervention is applied (B).
- **ABC assessment**: A type of FBA direct assessment in which the observer records every instance of the challenging behavior, including the time the behavior occurred, what happened just before the behavior, and what happened just after the behavior.
- **ABC checklist**: A variation of the ABC assessment with predefined antecedents, behaviors, and consequences.
- **Active student responding**: When a student emits a detectable response to ongoing instruction, such as saying, writing, or typing an answer.
- **Active supervision**: When the teacher actively looks around the classroom, moves around the classroom, and interacts with students to prevent instances of problem behaviors.
- **Alterable variables**: Things the teacher can change to produce improvements in students' learning and behaviors. These include the pace of teaching, responses to problem behaviors, and choice of materials.

❏ **Antecedents**: Stimuli that trigger challenging behaviors.

❏ **Applied behavior analysis (ABA)**: Application of the science of behavior analysis to improve socially significant behaviors. ABA emphasizes continuous measurement, close examination of the student's environment, and manipulation of antecedents and consequences to accomplish behavior change.

❏ **Behavior intervention plan (BIP)**: A written plan that describes procedures to prevent and reduce a student's challenging behaviors and how data will be used to evaluate these procedures. BIPs are designed for students who display chronic or intense challenging behaviors.

❏ **Behavior-specific praise**: Praise that provides information about the type, quality, or level of a student's behaviors.

❏ **Behavioral skills training (BST)**: A strategy to teach skills comprised of instructions, modeling of the skills, opportunities for practice, and performance-based feedback.

❏ **Board-certified behavior analyst (BCBA)**: A related-service provider with expertise in FBA and applied behavior analysis strategies.

❏ **Brisk instructional pacing**: When the teacher moves quickly through the lesson's content, minimizing downtime, while giving students sufficient wait-time to answer questions.

❏ **Check-in/check-out (CICO)** – A reinforcement system where students can earn points based on feedback about their behavior delivered via a daily behavior report card.

❏ **Choice making**: Providing students with an opportunity to make limited and reasonable choices in the context of classroom routines to promote self-determination and prosocial behaviors.

❏ **Choral responding**: When students vocally respond in unison to teacher-presented questions.

❏ **Classroom-wide token systems**: A type of independent group contingency in which the teacher makes the delivery of a reward contingent on each student earning a specified number of tokens, which are then exchanged for a backup reward.

❏ **Contextual fit**: Compatibility of the behavior intervention plan with variables in the educational environment.

❏ **Contingent praise and attention**: The application of praise and other forms of attention only when the student has performed specific academic, social, or other good behaviors.

❏ **Culture**: The socially learned behaviors, values, preferences, and knowledge specific to a group of people.

❏ **Culturally responsive practice**: Strategies that emphasize teachers' cultural knowledge and self-awareness, a commitment to supports that are relevant to their students' cultures and identities, and a focus on decision making to enhance culturally equitable outcomes.

❏ **Cultural self-awareness**: Understanding your own cultural perspectives, others' cultural perspectives, and how these affect your interactions.

❏ **Data**: Objective information about a behavior that enables a teacher to make informed decisions about PBS programming.

❏ **Data-based decision making**: The ongoing process of using data to determine how well the student is doing and to make program changes accordingly.

❏ **Dependent group contingencies**: A type of group contingency in which students earn rewards as a group contingent upon some or all of the group's behavior.

❏ **Differential reinforcement of low rates of behavior (DRL)**: Providing reinforcement if a challenging behavior occurs at or below a prespecified level during a fixed time period.

❏ **Differential reinforcement of other behavior (DRO)**: Providing reinforcement to the student after he has refrained from engaging in problem behaviors for a prespecified period of time.

❏ **Direct assessment**: Observing the student in settings where problem behaviors occur and collecting data to discover patterns between antecedents, behaviors, and consequences.

❏ **Discriminative stimulus (S^D)**: A stimulus, preceding a behavior, which signals that reinforcement is available for the behavior. SDs evoke behaviors that are followed by reinforcement.

❏ **Duration recording**: Recording the amount of time the student engages in a behavior.

❏ **Error correction**: When a teacher systematically responds to an error to increase the student's accuracy with a skill.

❏ **Event recording**: Tallying each time the student performs a behavior and then adding the tally marks to yield a frequency of the behavior per class period, session, or day.

❏ **Evidence-based practice (EBP)**: A model of decision making that relies on 1) the best available research evidence, 2) consumer values and context, and 3) clinical expertise.

❏ **Extinction**: When you stop delivering a reinforcer for a behavior and consequently the student performs the behavior less frequently.

❏ **Extinction burst**: When you stop delivering a reinforcer for a behavior and the frequency and/or intensity of a behavior initially increases before it decreases.

❏ **Formal indirect assessments**: Questionnaires and rating scales to systematically identify behavior functions.

❑ **Functional analysis**: Experimental manipulation of variables thought to maintain challenging behaviors for the purpose of identifying behavior functions.

❑ **Functional behavioral assessment (FBA)**: A collection of strategies to identify the environmental reasons why students engage in challenging behaviors for the purpose of developing effective interventions. These include indirect assessments, direct assessments, and functional analysis.

❑ **Functional behavioral assessment summary report**: A written report that summarizes information gained in each step of the FBA process, concluding with hypothesis statements for challenging behaviors.

❑ **Functional communication training (FCT)**: Teaching the student an alternative, appropriate response that produces the same reinforcing consequences as the problem behavior.

❑ **Good behavior game**: A type of dependent group contingency in which the class is divided into two teams who compete for a reward based upon which team displays the fewest problem behaviors.

❑ **Group contingencies**: Special reinforcement systems in which part or all of the class must perform appropriate behaviors to earn a reward.

❑ **Guided notes**: Handouts for lectures that allow students to write the key facts, concepts, and/or relationships being discussed in prepared spaces.

❑ **Independent group contingencies**: A type of group contingency in which each student earns rewards for her own behaviors.

❑ **Indirect assessment**: Interviewing people who know the student to gather information about variables maintaining problem behaviors.

❑ **Individual student schedule**: A personalized written or pictorial schedule that lists the activities a student is supposed to do throughout the school day.

❑ **Individualized education program (IEP)**: A written plan that describes how a student's special education program will be delivered and evaluated. Required components include present levels of performance, measurable goals and objectives, related services and accommodations, and how the child's progress will be documented.

❑ **Inter-trial interval**: The time period between the teacher's feedback and the next teacher-posed question.

❑ **Interval recording**: Dividing an observation period into equal intervals, and then recording whether the behavior occurs during each interval.

❑ **Latency recording**: Recording the time period between an instructional cue and when the student performs a behavior.

❏ **Momentary time sampling**: Dividing an observation period into equal intervals and then recording whether the behavior is occurring at the end of each interval.

❏ **Motivating operations (MOs)**: Events that alter the momentary value of reinforcers and the frequency of behaviors associated with those reinforcers.

❏ **Multicomponent interventions**: Simultaneously applying several interventions to prevent and eliminate problem behaviors.

❏ **Multi-tiered systems of support (MTSS)**: A model of service delivery in which students receive increasingly intensive levels of support based on their responsiveness to intervention.

❏ **Negative reinforcement**: When you remove something following a behavior that increases the likelihood that the behavior will occur again.

❏ **Neutralizing routine**: An intervention to reduce the reinforcing value of a problem behavior when an MO has occurred.

❏ **Non-alterable variables**: Things that affect students' learning and behaviors that are beyond the teacher's control (e.g., disabilities, genes, poverty).

❏ **Partial-interval recording**: A type of interval recording in which the behavior is recorded if it occurs during any part of the interval.

❏ **Positive behavior support (PBS)**: An approach to prevent and reduce challenging behavior through comprehensive lifestyle changes, a lifespan perspective, stakeholder participation, socially valid interventions, systems change, multicomponent interventions, prevention, flexibility with respect to scientific practices, and multiple theoretical perspectives. Also known as positive behavioral interventions and supports (PBIS).

❏ **Positive reinforcement**: When you add something following a behavior that increases the likelihood that the behavior will occur again.

❏ **Precorrections**: Reminders for students to engage in appropriate behaviors and to refrain from inappropriate behaviors.

❏ **Premack principle**: An application of positive reinforcement, in which the opportunity to engage in a higher probability behavior reinforces a lower probability behavior.

❏ **Procedural fidelity**: The extent to which procedures in the written BIP are implemented as described.

❏ **Prompt**: A supplemental discriminative stimulus (SD), or other forms of assistance, to produce a desired behavior.

❏ **Punishment**: Any event following a behavior that decreases the likelihood that the behavior will occur in the future.

❏ **Rate recording**: A variation of event recording in which the total frequency of a behavior is divided by a unit of time (e.g., minutes, hours).

❏ **Reinforcement**: Any event following a behavior that increases the likelihood that the behavior will occur again.

❏ **Response cards**: Blank or preprinted cards on which students write or select answers during teacher-directed lessons.

❏ **Response to intervention (RTI)**: A multi-tiered approach that emphasizes prevention of academic failure through early screening and intervention.

❏ **Risk index**: The percentage of members of a group experiencing a particular outcome.

❏ **Risk ratio**: The likelihood of an outcome in one group relative to another group, calculated by dividing the risk index of a target group by the risk index of a comparison group.

❏ **Scatter plot**: a type of FBA direct assessment that uses a grid to identify patterns in problem behaviors across time.

❏ **School-Wide PBIS Culturally Responsive Tiered Fidelity Inventory (CR-TFI)**: A tool to address the fidelity of SWPBIS implementation that includes cultural considerations.

❏ **School-Wide Positive Behavioral Interventions and Supports (SWPBIS)**: An application of PBS in schools that emphasizes systems of support at primary, secondary, and tertiary levels.

❏ **Teaching students to recruit teacher attention**: Instructions, prompts, and reinforcement to help students independently get the teacher's attention when they have completed their work or need help from the teacher to complete their work.

❏ **Thinning the schedule of reinforcement**: The process of gradually decreasing how frequently you deliver reinforcement (e.g., praise, rewards) to a student. This can be accomplished by increasing the number of responses required to earn reinforcement or by increasing the amount of time with appropriate behavior that must pass before the student earns reinforcement.

❏ **Three-term contingency of behavior**: When S^D is presented, which evokes a behavior, that is followed by reinforcement.

❏ **Wait-time**: The interval between when the teacher asks a question and the student responds, usually controlled by a cue from the teacher.

❏ **Whole class schedule**: A publicly posted schedule that depicts what the entire class is doing throughout the school day.

❏ **Whole-interval recording**: A type of interval recording in which the behavior is recorded if it occurs during the entire interval.

References

Alber, S. R., & Heward, W. L. (1997). Recruit it or lose it!: Training students to recruit positive teacher attention. *Intervention in School and Clinic, 32,* 275–282. https://doi.org/10.1177/105345129703200504

Alber, S. R., Heward, W. L., & Hippler, B. J. (1999). Teaching middle school students with learning disabilities to recruit positive teacher attention. *Exceptional Children, 65,* 253–270. https://doi.org/10.1177/001440299906500209

Alberto, P. A., Troutman, A. C., & Axe, J. (2020). *Applied behavior analysis for teachers* (10th ed.). Pearson.

Albin, R. W., Luchyshyn, J. M., Horner, R. H., & Flannery, K. B. (1996). Contextual fit for behavioral support plans: A model for "goodness of fit." In L. Koegel, R. Koegel, & G. Dunlap (Eds.), *Positive behavioral support: Including people with difficult behavior in the community.* Baltimore, MD: Paul Hl Brookes.

Algozzine, B., Barrett, S., Eber, L., George, H., Horner, R., Lewis, T., Putnam, B., Swain-Bradway, J., McIntosh, K., & Sugai, G. (2014). *Culturally Responsive School-wide PBIS Tiered Fidelity Inventory.* OSEP Technical Assistance Center on Positive Behavioral Interventions and Supports.

Alter, P., & Haydon, T. (2017). Characteristics of effective classroom rules: A review of the literature. *Teacher Education and Special Education, 40,* 114–127. https://doi.org/10.1177/0888406417700962

Arden, S. V., Gandhi, A. G., Zumeta Edmonds, R., & Danielson, L. (2017). Toward more effective tiered systems: Lessons from national implementation efforts. *Exceptional Children, 83*, 269–280.

Barbetta, P., & Heward, W. (1993). Effects of active student response during error correction on the acquisition and maintenance of geography facts by elementary students with learning disabilities. *Journal of Behavioral Education, 3*, 217–233. https://doi.org/10.1007/BF00961552

Barbetta, P., Heron, T., & Heward, W. (1993). Effects of active student response during error correction on the acquisition, maintenance, and generalization of sight words by students with developmental disabilities. *Journal of Applied Behavior Analysis, 26*, 111–119. https://doi.org/10.1901/jaba.1993.26-111

Barrish, H., Saunders, M., & Wolf, M. (1969). Good behavior game: Effects of individual contingencies for group consequences on disruptive behavior in a classroom. *Journal of Applied Behavior Analysis, 2*, 119–124. https://doi.org/10.1901/jaba.1969.2-119

Bal, A. (2018). Culturally responsive positive behavioral interventions and supports: A process–oriented framework for systemic transformation. *Review of Education, Pedagogy, and Cultural Studies, 40*(2), 144–174. https://doi.org/10.1080/10714413.2017.1417579

Bayat, M., Mindes, G., & Covitt, S. (2010). What does RTI (response to intervention) look like in preschool? *Early Childhood Education Journal, 37*, 493–500. https://doi.org/10.1007/s10643-010-0372-6

Benazzi, L., Horner, R. H., & Good, R. H. (2006). Effects of behavior support team composition on the technical adequacy and contextual fit of behavior support plans. *The Journal of Special Education, 40*, 160–170. https://doi.org/10.1177/00224669060400030401

Bijou, S. W., Peterson, R. F., & Ault, M. H. (1968). A method to integrate descriptive and experimental field studies at the level of data and empirical concept. *Journal of Applied Behavior Analysis, 1*, 175–191. https://doi.org/10.1901/jaba.1968.1-175

Birukou A., Blanzieri E., Giorgini P., & Giunchiglia F. (2013) A formal definition of culture. In K. Sycara, M. Gelfand, & A. Abbe (Eds.) *Models for intercultural collaboration and negotiation. Advances in group decision and negotiation*, vol. 6, 1–26. Dordrecht: Springer. https://doi.org/10.1007/978-94-007-5574-1_1

Bloom, B. S. (1980). The new direction in educational research: Alterable variables. *Phi Delta Kappan, 61*, 382–385.

Bondy, A. H., & Tincani, M. (2018). Effects of response cards on students with autism spectrum disorder or intellectual disability. *Education and Training in Autism and Developmental Disabilities, 53*, 59–72.

Butler, L., & Luiselli, J. (2007). Escape-maintained problem behavior in a child with autism: Antecedent functional analysis and intervention evaluation of noncontingent escape and instructional fading. *Journal of Positive Behavior Interventions, 9,* 195–202. https://doi.org/10.1177/10983007070 090040201

Brady, L., Padden, C., & McGill, P. (2019). Improving procedural fidelity of behavioural interventions for people with intellectual and developmental disabilities: A systematic review. *Journal of Applied Research in Intellectual Disabilities, 32,* 762–778. https://doi.org/10.1111/jar.12585

Brunsting, N. C., Sreckovic, M. A., & Lane, K. L. (2014). Special education teacher burnout: A synthesis of research from 1979 to 2013. *Education and Treatment of Children, 37*(4), 681–711. http://doi.org/10.1353/etc .2014.0032

Carr, E. G., Dunlap, G., Horner, R. H., Koegel, R. L., Turnbull, A. P., Sailor, W., et al. (2002). Positive behavior support: Evolution of an applied science. *Journal of Positive Behavior Interventions, 4,* 4–16, 20. https://doi.org/10 .1177/109830070200400102

Cameron, J., & Pierce, W. (1994). Reinforcement, reward, and intrinsic motivation: A meta-analysis. *Review of Educational Research, 64*(3), 363–423. https://doi.org/10.2307/1170677

Campbell, A., & Anderson, C. M. (2008). Enhancing effects of check-in/check-out with function-based support. *Behavioral Disorders, 33,* 233–245. https://doi.org/10.1177/019874290803300404

Campbell, R. V., & Lutzker, J. R. (1993). Using functional equivalence training to reduce severe challenging behavior: A case study. *Journal of Developmental and Physical Disabilities, 5,* 203–216. https://doi.org/1056-263x/93/0900 -0203507.00

Cannella, H., O'Reilly, M., & Lancioni, G. (2006). Treatment of hand mouthing in individuals with severe to profound developmental disabilities: A review of the literature. *Research in Developmental Disabilities, 2,* 529–544. https://doi.org/10.1016/j.ridd.2005.06.004

Carnine, D. W. (1976). Effects of two teacher-presentation rates on off-task behavior, answering correctly, and participation. *Journal of Applied Behavior Analysis, 9,* 199–206. https://doi.org/10.1901/jaba.1976.9-199

Carr, E. G., & Durrand, V. M. (1985). Reducing problem behaviors through functional communication training. *Journal of Applied Behavior Analysis, 18,* 111–126. https://doi.org/10.1901/jaba.1985.18-111

Carter, D., & Horner, R. (2009). Adding function-based behavioral support to first step to success: Integrating individualized and manualized practices. *Journal of Positive Behavior Interventions, 11,* 22–34. https://doi.org/10.1177 /1098300708319125

Carter, D., & Horner, R. (2007). Adding functional behavioral assessment to first step to success: A case study. *Journal of Positive Behavior Interventions, 9,* 229–238. https://doi.org/10.1177/10983007070090040501

Cholewa, B., Hull, M. F., Babcock, C. R., & Smith, A. D. (2018). Predictors and academic outcomes associated with in-school suspension. *School Psychology Quarterly, 33*, 191. https://doi.org/10.1037/spq0000213

Clunies-Ross, P., Little, E., & Kienhuis, M. (2008). Self-reported and actual use of proactive and reactive classroom management strategies and their relationship with teacher stress and student behaviour. *Educational Psychology, 28*, 693–710. https://doi.org/10.1080/01443410802206700

Colvin, G., Sugai, G., Good, R., & Lee, Y. (1997). Using active supervision and precorrection to improve transition behaviors in an elementary school. *School Psychology Quarterly, 12*, 344–363. https://doi.org/10.1037/h0088967

Cook, B. G., & Odom, S. L. (2013). Evidence-based practices and implementation science in special education. *Exceptional Children, 79*, 135–144. https://doi.org/10.1177/001440291307900201

Conroy, M., & Stichter, J. (2003). The application of antecedents in the functional assessment process: Existing research, issues, and recommendations. *The Journal of Special Education, 37*, 15–25. https://doi.org/10.1177/00224669030370010201

Conroy, M., Sutherland, K., Snyder, A., & Marsh, S. (2008). Classwide interventions: Effective instruction makes a difference. *Teaching Exceptional Children, 4*, 24–30. https://doi.org/10.1177/004005990804000603

Cooper, J. O., Heron, T. E., & Heward, W. L. (2020). *Applied behavior analysis* (3rd ed). Pearson.

Craft, M., Alber, S., & Heward, W. (1998). Teaching elementary students with developmental disabilities to recruit teacher attention in a general education classroom: Effects on teacher praise and academic productivity. *Journal of Applied Behavior Analysis, 31*, 399–415. https://doi.org/10.1901/jaba.1998.31-399

Crone, D. A., Hawken, L. S., & Horner, R. H. (2010). *Responding to problem behavior in schools: The behavior education program* (2nd ed.). New York, NY: Guilford Press.

Crozier, S., & Tincani, M. (2007). Effects of social stories on prosocial behavior of preschool children with autism spectrum disorders. *Journal of Autism and Developmental Disorders, 37*, 1803–1814. http://doi.org/10.1007/s10803-006-0315-7

De Pry, R. L., & Sugai, G. (2002). The effect of active supervision and pre-correction on minor behavioral incidents in a sixth grade general education classroom. *Journal of Behavioral Education, 11*, 255–267. https://doi.org/10.1023/A:1021162906622

Dietz, S. M., & Repp, A. C. (1973). Decreasing classroom misbehavior through use of DRL schedules of reinforcement. *Journal of Applied Behavior Analysis, 6*, 457–463. https://doi.org/10.1901/jaba.1973.6-457

Dolan, L. J., Kellam, S. G., Brown, C. H., & Werthamer-Larsson, L., Rebok, G. W., Mayer, L. S., et al. (1993). The short-term impact of two classroom-based preventive interventions on aggressive and shy behaviors and poor achievement. *Journal of Applied Developmental Psychology, 14,* 317–345. https://doi.org/10.1016/0193-3973(93)90013-L

Douglas, K. H., & Uphold, N. M. (2014). iPad® or iPod touch®: Evaluating self-created electronic photographic activity schedules and student preferences. *Journal of Special Education Technology, 29,* 1–14. https://doi.org/10.1177/016264341402900301

Duncan, A. (2009). Teacher preparation: Reforming the uncertain profession—Remarks of Secretary Arne Duncan at Teachers College, Columbia University. http://www.tc.columbia.edu/news/article.htm?id=7195

Dunlap G., & Fox, L. (1999). A demonstration of positive behavioral support for young children with autism. *Journal of Positive Behavioral Interventions, 1,* 77–87. https://doi.org/10.1177/109830079900100202

Dunlap, G., Hieneman, M., Knoster, T., Fox, L., Anderson, J., & Albin, R. W. (2000). Essential elements of inservice training in positive behavior support. *Journal of Positive Behavior Interventions, 2,* 22–32. https://doi.org/10.1177/109830070000200104

Dunlap, G., Carr, E., Horner, R., Zarcone, J., & Schwartz, I. (2008). Positive behavior support and applied behavior analysis: A familial alliance. *Behavior Modification, 32,* 682–698. https://doi.org/10.1177/0145445508317132

Dunlap, G., Ester, T., Langhans, S., & Fox, L. (2006). Functional communication training with toddlers in home environments. *Journal of Early Intervention, 28,* 81–96. https://doi.org/10.1177/105381510602800201

Dunlap, G., Kincaid, D., Horner, R. H., Knoster, T., & Bradshaw, C. P. (2014). A comment on the term "positive behavior support". *Journal of Positive Behavior Interventions, 16,* 133–136. https://doi.org/10.1177/1098300713497099

Dunlap, G., Strain, P., Lee, J. K., Joseph, J., & Leech, N. (2018). A randomized controlled evaluation of prevent-teach-reinforce for young children. *Topics in Early Childhood Special Education, 37,* 195–205. https://doi.org/10.1177/0271121417724874

Durand, V. M., & Carr, E. G. (1991). Functional communication training to reduce challenging behavior: Maintenance and application in new settings. *Journal of Applied Behavior Analysis, 24,* 251–264. https://doi-org./10.1901/jaba.1991.24-251

Durand, V. M., & Crimmins, D. B. (1988). *The motivation assessment scale.* Topeka: Monaco & Associates.

Durand, V. M. & Merges, E. (2001). Functional communication training: A contemporary behavior analytic intervention for problem behavior. *Focus*

on *Autism and Other Developmental Disabilities, 16,* 110–119. https://doi
.org/10.1177/108835760101600207

Ellis, J., & Magee, S. K. (1999). Determination of environmental correlates of
disruptive classroom behavior: Integration of functional analysis into public
school assessment process. *Education & Treatment of Children (ETC), 22,*
291–316.

Feeney, T., & Ylvisaker, M. (2003). Context-sensitive behavioral supports for
young children with TBI: Short-term effects and long-term outcome. *The
Journal of Head Trauma Rehabilitation, 18,* 33–51.

Fisher, W., Piazza, C., Cataldo, M., & Harrell, R. (1993). Functional communication training with and without extinction and punishment. *Journal of Applied
Behavior Analysis, 26,* 23–36. https://doi.org/10.1901/jaba.1993.26-23

Flower, A., McKenna, J. W., & Haring, C. D. (2017). Behavior and classroom
management: Are teacher preparation programs really preparing our
teachers? *Preventing School Failure: Alternative Education for Children and
Youth, 61,* 163–169. https://doi.org/10.1080/1045988X.2016.1231109

Fuchs, D., & Deshler, D. (2007). What we need to know About responsiveness to
intervention (and shouldn't be afraid to ask). *Learning Disabilities Research
& Practice, 22,* 129–136. https://doi.org/10.1111/j.1540-5826.2007.00237.x

Fuchs, D., & Fuchs, L. (2008). Implementing RTI. *District Administration,
44*(11), 72–76.

Gage, N. A., Leite, W., Childs, K., & Kincaid, D. (2017). Average treatment
effect of school-wide positive behavioral interventions and supports on
school-level academic achievement in Florida. *Journal of Positive Behavior
Interventions, 19,* 158–167. https://doi.org/10.1177/1098300717693556

Gage, N. A., Whitford, D. K., & Katsiyannis, A. (2018). A review of schoolwide
positive behavior interventions and supports as a framework for reducing
disciplinary exclusions. *The Journal of Special Education, 52,* 142–151.
https://doi.org/10.1177/0022466918767847

Gardner, R., Bird, F., Maguire, H., Carreiro, R., & Abenaim, N. (2003). Intensive
positive behavior supports for adolescents with acquired brain injury:
Long-term outcomes in community settings. *The Journal of Head Trauma
Rehabilitation, 18,* 52–74. https://doi.org/10.1097/00001199-200301000
-00007

Ghaemmaghami, M., Hanley, G. P., & Jessel, J. (2021). Functional communication training: From efficacy to effectiveness. *Journal of Applied Behavior
Analysis, 54,* 122–143. http://doi: 10.1002/jaba.762

Gillespie-Lynch, K., Kapp, S. K., Brooks, P. J., Pickens, J., & Schwartzman, B.
(2017). Whose expertise is it? Evidence for autistic adults as critical autism
experts. *Frontiers in Psychology, 8,* 438. https://doi.org/10.3389/fpsyg.2017
.00438

Gilmour, A. F. (2018). Has inclusion gone too far? Weighing its effects on students with disabilities, their peers, and teachers. *Education Next, 18*(4), 8–17. https://www.educationnext.org/has-inclusion-gone-too-far-weighing-effects-students-with-disabilities-peers-teachers/

Gilmour, A. F., Fuchs, D., & Wehby, J. H. (2019). Are students with disabilities accessing the curriculum? A meta-analysis of the reading achievement gap between students with and without disabilities. *Exceptional Children, 85*, 329–346. https://doi.org/10.1177/0014402918795830

Goh, A. E., & Bambara, L. M. (2012). Individualized positive behavior support in school settings: A meta-analysis. *Remedial and Special Education, 33*, 271–286. https://doi.org/10.1177/0741932510383990

Graham-Day, K. J., Gardner III, R., & Hsin, Y. W. (2010). Increasing on-task behaviors of high school students with attention deficit hyperactivity disorder: Is it enough?. *Education and Treatment of Children, 33*, 205–221. https://www.jstor.org/stable/42900063

Gregory, A., Skiba, R. J., & Noguera, P. A. (2010). The achievement gap and the discipline gap: Two sides of the same coin? *Educational Researcher, 39*, 59–68. https://doi.org/10.3102/0013189X09357621

Gresham, F. M. (1989). Assessment of treatment integrity in school consultation and prereferral intervention. *School Psychology Review, 18*, 37–50. https://doi.org/10.1080/02796015.1989.12085399

Greenwood, C., Hops, H., Delquadri, J., & Guild, J. (1974). Group contingencies for group consequences in classroom management: A further analysis. *Journal of Applied Behavior Analysis, 7*, 413–425. https://doi.org/10.1901/jaba.1974.7-413

Greenwood, C. R., Delquadri, J., & Hall, R. V. (1984). Opportunity to respond and student academic achievement. In W. L. Heward, T. E. Heron, D. S. Hill, & D. Trap-Porter (Eds.), *Focus on behavior analysis in education* (pp. 58–88). Indianapolis, IN: Merrill.

Grskovic, J., & Belfiore, P. (1996). Improving the spelling performance of students with disabilities. *Journal of Behavioral Education, 6*, 343–354. https://www.jstor.org/stable/41824136

Haley, J. L., Heick, P. F., & Luiselli, J. K. (2010). Use of an antecedent intervention to decrease vocal stereotypy of a student with autism in the general education classroom. *Child & Family Behavior Therapy, 32*, 311–321. https://doi.org/10.1080/07317107.2010.515527

Hall, R. V., Lund, D., & Jackson, D. (1968). Effects of teacher attention on study behavior *Journal of Applied Behavior Analysis, 1*, 1–12. https://doi.org/10.1901/jaba.1968.1-1

Heinicke, M. R., Carr, J. E., Mozzoni, M. P., & Roane, H. (2009). Using differential reinforcement to decrease academic response latencies of an adolescent with acquired brain injury. *Journal of Applied Behavior Analysis, 42,* 861–865. https://doi.org/10.1901/jaba.2009.42-861

Horner, R., Dunlap, G., Koegel, R., & Carr, E. (1990). Toward a technology of 'nonaversive' behavioral support. *Journal of the Association for Persons with Severe Handicaps, 30,* 125–132. https://doi.org/10.1177/154079699001500301

Horner, R. H., & Sugai, G. (2015). School-wide PBIS: An example of applied behavior analysis implemented at a scale of social importance. *Behavior Analysis in Practice, 8,* 80–85. https://doi.org/10.1007/s40617-015-0045-4

Horner, R., Sugai, G., Smolkowski, K., Eber, L., Nakasato, J., Todd, A., et al. (2009). A randomized, wait-list controlled effectiveness trial assessing school-wide positive behavior support in elementary schools. *Journal of Positive Behavior Interventions, 11,* 133–144. https://doi.org/10.1177/1098300709332067

Horner, R. H., Vaughn, B. J., Day, H. M., & Ard, W. R. (1996). The relationship between setting events and problem behavior: Expanding our understanding of behavioral support. In L. K. Koegel, R. L. Koegel, & G. Dunlap (Eds.), *Positive behavioral support: Including people with difficult behavior in the community* (pp. 381–402). Baltimore: Brookes.

Hulac, D. M., & Benson, N. (2010). The use of group contingencies for preventing and managing disruptive behaviors. *Intervention in School and Clinic, 45,* 257–262. https://doi.org/10.1177/1053451209353442

Iovannone, R., Anderson, C., & Scott, T. (2017). Understanding setting events: What they are and how to identify them. *Beyond Behavior, 26,* 105–112. https://doi.org/10.1177/1074295617729795

Joslyn, P. R., Donaldson, J. M., Austin, J. L., & Vollmer, T. R. (2019). The good behavior game: A brief review. *Journal of Applied Behavior Analysis, 52,* 811–815. https://doi.org/10.1002/jaba.572

Johnson-Gros, K., Lyons, E., & Griffin, R. (2008). Active supervision: An intervention to reduce high school tardiness. *Education & Treatment of Children, 31,* 39–53. https://www.jstor.org/stable/42899962

Kern, L., & Clemens, N. (2007). Antecedent strategies to promote appropriate classroom behavior. *Psychology in the Schools, 44,* 65–75. https://doi.org/10.1002/pits.20206

Kohn, A. (1999). Punished by rewards: The trouble with gold stars. *Incentive plans, a's, praise, and other bribes.* Boston, MA: Houghton Mifflin Harcourt.

Kokkinos, C. (2007). Job stressors, personality and burnout in primary school teachers. *British Journal of Educational Psychology, 77,* 229–243. https://doi.org/10.1348/000709905X90344

Kirkpatrick, M., Akers, J., & Rivera, G. (2019). Use of behavioral skills training with teachers: A systematic review. *Journal of Behavioral Education, 28,* 344–361. https://doi.org/10.1007/s10864-019-09322-z

Knight, V. F., Huber, H. B., Kuntz, E. M., Carter, E. W., & Juarez, A. P. (2019). Instructional practices, priorities, and preparedness for educating students with autism and intellectual disability. *Focus on Autism and Other Developmental Disabilities, 34*, 3–14. https://doi.org/10.1177/1088357618755694

Konrad, M., Joseph, L., & Eveleigh, E. (2009). Meta-analytic review of guided notes. *Education & Treatment of Children, 32*, 421–444. https://doi.org/10.1353/etc.0.0066

Laraway, S., Snycerski, S., Michael, J., & Poling, A. (2003). Motivating operations and terms to describe them: Some further refinements. *Journal of Applied Behavior Analysis, 36*, 407–414. https://doi.org/10.1901/jaba.2003.36-407

Lee, J. (2002). Racial and ethnic achievement gap trends: Reversing the progress toward equity? *Educational Researcher, 31*, 3–12. https://doi.org/10.3102/0013189X031001003

Lee, D. L., & Axelrod, S. (2005). *Behavior modification: Basic principles.* Pro-Ed.

Leverson, M., Smith, K., McIntosh, K., Rose, J., & Pinkelman, S. (2016). *PBIS cultural responsiveness field guide: Resources for trainers and coaches.* Office of Special Education Programs Technical Assistance Center on Positive Behavioral Interventions and Supports. https://www.pbis.org/resource/pbis-cultural-responsiveness-field-guide-resources-for-trainers-and-coaches

Morgan, P. L., Farkas, G., Hillemeier, M. M., Wang, Y., Mandel, Z., DeJarnett, C., & Maczuga, S. (2019). Are students with disabilities suspended more frequently than otherwise similar students without disabilities? *Journal of School Psychology, 72*, 1–13. https://doi.org/10.1016/j.jsp.2018.11.001

McIntosh, K., Barnes, A., Eliason, B., & Morris, K. (2014). *Using discipline data within SWPBIS to identify and address disproportionality: A guide for school teams.* OSEP Technical Assistance Center on Positive Behavioral Interventions and Supports. https://www.pbis.org/resource/using-discipline-data-within-swpbis-to-identify-and-address-disproportionality-a-guide-for-school-teams

O'Brennan, L., Pas, E., & Bradshaw, C. (2017). Multilevel examination of burnout among high school staff: Importance of staff and school factors. *School Psychology Review, 46*, 165–176. https://doi.org/10.17105/SPR-2015-0019.V46-2

O'Dell, S. M., Vilardo, B. A., Kern, L., Kokina, A., Ash, A. N., Seymour, K. J., et al. (2011). JPBI 10 years later: Trends in research studies. *Journal of Positive Behavior Interventions, 13*, 78–86. https://doi.org/10.1177/1098300717722359

OSEP Technical Assistance Center on PBIS (2021). *Getting started.* https://www.pbis.org/pbis/getting-started

Pomerance, L., & Walsh, K. (2020). *2020 teacher prep review: Clinical practice and classroom management.* Washington, DC: National Council on Teacher Quality. Retrieved from: www.nctq.org/publications/2020-Teacher-Prep-Review:-Clinical-Practice-and-Classroom-Management

Harris, V., & Sherman, J. (1973). Use and analysis of the 'good behavior game' to reduce disruptive classroom behavior. *Journal of Applied Behavior Analysis, 6*(3), 405–417. https://doi.org/10.1901/jaba.1973.6-405

Haydon, T., Mancil, G., & Van Loan, C. (2009). Using opportunities to respond in a general education classroom: A case study. *Education & Treatment of Children, 32*, 267–278. https://www.jstor.org/stable/42900022

Heron, T. E., & Harris, K. C. (2001). *The educational consultant: Helping professionals, parents, and students in inclusive classrooms* (4th ed.). Pro-Ed.

Heron, T. E., Hippler, B., & Tincani, M. (2003). How to help students complete classwork and homework assignments. In S. Axelrod, & S. Mathews (Eds.), *How to improve classroom behavior series.* Pro-Ed.

Heward, W. L. (2003). Ten faculty notions about teaching and learning that hinder the effectiveness of special education. *The Journal of Special Education, 36*, 186–205. https://doi.org/10.1177/002246690303600401

Heward, W. L. (1994). Three low-tech strategies for increasing the frequency of active student response during group instruction. In R. Gardner III, Sainato, D., Cooper, J. O., Heron, T., Heward, W. L., Eshleman, J., & T. A. Grossi. (Eds.) *Behavior analysis in education: Focus on measurable superior instruction* (pp. 283–320). Pacific Grove, CA: Brooks/Cole.

Horner, R., Day, H., & Day, J. (1997). Using neutralizing routines to reduce problem behaviors. *Journal of Applied Behavior Analysis, 30*, 601–614. https://doi.org/10.1901/jaba.1997.30-601

Iwata, B. A., & DeLeon, I. G. (2005). *The functional analysis screening tool (FAST).* Gainesville, FL: The Florida Center on Self-Injury, University of Florida. https://doi.org/10.1177/10534512050400030101

Iwata, B. A., Dorsey, M., Slifer, K., Bauman, K., & Richman, G. (1982/1994). Towards a functional analysis of self-injury. *Analysis and Intervention in Developmental Disabilities, 2*, 3–20. [Reprinted in *Journal of Applied Behavior Analysis, 27*, 197–209]. https://doi.org/10.1901/jaba.1994.27-197

Johnson, T., Stoner, G., & Green, S. (1996). Demonstrating the experimenting society model with classwide behavior management interventions. *School Psychology Review, 25*, 199–214. https://doi.org/10.1080/02796015.1996.12085811

Lalli, J., Pinter-Lalli, E., Mace, F., & Murphy, D. (1991). Training interactional behaviors of adults with developmental disabilities: A systematic replication and extension. *Journal of Applied Behavior Analysis, 24*, 167–174. https://doi.org/10.1901/jaba.1991.24-167

Lambert, M., Cartledge, G., Heward, W., & Lo, Y. (2006). Effects of response cards on disruptive behavior and academic responding during math lessons by fourth-grade urban students. *Journal of Positive Behavior Interventions, 8*, 88–99. https://doi.org/10.1177/10983007060080020701

Luiselli, J., Dunn, E., & Pace, G. (2005). Antecedent assessment and intervention to reduce physical restraint (protective holding) of children and adolescents with acquired brain injury. *Behavioral Interventions, 20*, 51–65. https://doi.org/10.1002/bin.170

Maag, J. (2001). Rewarded by punishment: Reflections on the disuse of positive reinforcement in schools. *Exceptional Children, 67*, 173–186. https://doi.org/10.1177/001440290106700203

MacSuga-Gage, A. S., & Simonsen, B. (2015). Examining the effects of teacher-directed opportunities to respond on student outcomes: A systematic review of the literature. *Education and Treatment of Children, 38*, 211–239. https://doi.org/10.1353/etc.2015.0009

Maggin, D. M., Zurheide, J., Pickett, K. C., & Baillie, S. J. (2015). A systematic evidence review of the check-in/check-out program for reducing student challenging behaviors. *Journal of Positive Behavior Interventions, 17*, 197–208. https://doi.org/10.1177/1098300715573630

Maheady, L., Sacca, M. K., Harper, G. F. (1987). Classwide student tutoring teams: The effects of peer-mediated instruction on the academic performance of secondary mainstreamed students. *Journal of Special Education, 21*, 107–21. https://doi.org/10.1177/002246698702100309

March, R. E., Horner, R. H., Lewis-Palmer, T., Brown, D., Crone, D., Todd, A. W., et al. (2000). *Functional assessment checklist: Teachers and staff (FACTS)*. Eugene, OR: Educational and Community Supports.

Marquis, J. G., Horner, R. H., Carr, E. G., Turnbull, A. P., Thompson, M., Behrens, G. A., et al. (2000). A meta-analysis of positive behavior support. *Contemporary Special Education Research: Syntheses of the Knowledge Base on Critical Instructional Issues, 11*, 137–178.

Massey, N., & Wheeler, J. (2000). Acquisition and generalization of activity schedules and their effects on task engagement in a young child with autism in an inclusive pre–school classroom. *Education & Training in Mental Retardation & Developmental Disabilities, 35*, 326–335.

Mayer, M., Reyes-Guzman, C., Grana, R., Choi, K., & Freedman, N. D. (2020). Demographic characteristics, cigarette smoking, and e-cigarette use among US adults. *JAMA Network Open, 3*(10), e2020694–e2020694. https://doi:10.1001/jamanetworkopen.2020.20694

McIntosh, K., Gion, C., & Bastable, E. (2018). Do schools implementing SWPBIS have decreased racial and ethnic disproportionality in school discipline? *PBIS Evaluation Brief*. OSEP National Technical Assistance Center on Positive Behavioral Interventions and Supports. https://www

.pbis.org/resource/do-schools-implementing-swpbis-have-decreased-racial
-and-ethnic-disproportionality-in-school-discipline

Mitchell, A., & Arnold, M. (2004). Behavior management skills as predictors of retention among South Texas Special Educators. *Journal of Instructional Psychology, 31,* 214–219.

Morris, E. W., & Perry, B. L. (2016). The punishment gap: School suspension and racial disparities in achievement. *Social Problems, 63,* 68–86. https:// doi.org/10.1093/socpro/spv026

National Center for Education Statistics. (2000). *Schools and staffing survey (SASS), "Public teacher questionnaire," 1993–94 and 1999–2000.* Washington, DC: U.S. Department of Education.

Noguera, P. A. (2008). Creating schools where race does not predict achievement: The role and significance of race in the racial achievement gap. *The Journal of Negro Education, 77,* 90–103. http://www.jstor.org/stable /25608673

Oliver, R. M., Wehby, J. H., & Reschly, D. J. (2011). Teacher classroom management practices: Effects on disruptive or aggressive student behavior. *Campbell Systematic Reviews, 7,* 1–55. https://doi.org/10.4073/csr.2011.4

O'Neill, R. E., Albin, R. W., Storey, K Horner, R. H., & Sprague, J. R. (2015). *Functional assessment and program development for problem behavior: A practical handbook* (3rd ed.). Cengage Learning.

Paclawskyj, T. R., Matson, J. L., Rush, K. S., Smalls, Y., & Vollmer, T. R. (2000). Questions about behavioral function (QABF): A behavioral checklist for functional assessment of aberrant behavior. *Research in Developmental Disabilities, 21,* 223–229. https://doi.org/10.1016/S0891-4222(00)00036-6

Pisacreta, J., Tincani, M., Connell, J. E., & Axelrod, S. (2011). Increasing teachers' use of a 1: 1 praise-to-behavior correction ratio to decrease student disruption in general education classrooms. *Behavioral Interventions, 26,* 243–260. https://doi.org/10.1002/bin.341

Poling, A., & Ryan, C. (1982). Differential-reinforcement-of-other-behavior schedules: Therapeutic applications. *Behavior Modification, 6,* 3–21. https://doi.org/10.1177/01454455820061001

Premack, D. (1963). Rate differential reinforcement in monkey manipulation. *Journal of the Experimental Analysis of Behavior, 6,* 81–89. https://doi.org /10.1901/jeab.1963.6-81

Rattan, S., & Wrightington, M. (2020). Premack's principle and visual schedules. In M. Axelrod, M. Coolong-Chaffin, & R. O. Hawkins (Eds.), *School-based behavioral intervention case studies* (pp. 62–75). Routledge.

Rapp, J. T., Colby-Dirksen, A. M., Michalski, D. N., Carroll, R. A., & Lindenberg, A. M. (2008). Detecting changes in simulated events using partial-interval recording and momentary time sampling. *Behavioral Interventions: Theory*

& Practice in Residential & Community-Based Clinical Programs, 23, 237–269. https://doi.org/10.1002/bin.269

Ray, K., & Watson, T. (2001). Analysis of the effects of temporally distant events on school behavior. *School Psychology Quarterly, 16*, 324–342. https://doi .org/10.1521/scpq.16.3.324.19891

Rispoli, M., Ninci, J., Neely, L., & Zaini, S. (2014). A systematic review of trial-based functional analysis of challenging behavior. *Journal of Developmental and Physical Disabilities, 26*(3), 271–283. https://doi.org/10.1007/s10882 -013-9363-z

Rosenfield, P., Lambert, N., & Black, A. (1985). Desk arrangement effects on pupil classroom behavior. *Journal of Educational Psychology, 77*, 101–108. https://doi.org/10.1037/0022-0663.77.1.101

Rossetti, Z., Sauer, J. S., Bui, O., & Ou, S. (2017). Developing collaborative partnerships with culturally and linguistically diverse families during the IEP process. *Teaching Exceptional Children, 49*, 328–338. https://doi.org/10 .1177/0040059918758163

Rouse, C. A., Everhart-Sherwood, J. M., & Alber-Morgan, S. R. (2014). Effects of self-monitoring and recruiting teacher attention on pre-vocational skills. *Education and Training in Autism and Developmental Disabilities, 49*, 313–327. https://www.jstor.org/stable/23880613

Royer, D. J., Lane, K. L., Dunlap, K. D., & Ennis, R. P. (2019). A systematic review of teacher-delivered behavior-specific praise on K–12 student performance. *Remedial and Special Education, 40*, 112–128. https://doi.org/10.1177 /0741932517751054

Rubow, C. C., Vollmer, T. R., & Joslyn, P. R. (2018). Effects of the good behavior game on student and teacher behavior in an alternative school. *Journal of Applied Behavior Analysis, 51*, 382–392. https://doi.org/10.1002/jaba.455

Sarokoff, R. A., & Sturmey, P. (2004). The effects of behavioral skills training on staff implementation of discrete-trial teaching. *Journal of Applied Behavior Analysis, 37*, 535–538. https://doi.org/10.1901/jaba.2004.37-535

Scott, T., Anderson, C., & Spaulding, S. (2008). Strategies for developing and carrying out functional assessment and behavior intervention planning. *Preventing School Failure, 52*, 39–49. https://doi.org/10.3200/PSFL.52.3 .39-50

Schwartz, I. S., & Baer, D. M. (1991). Social validity assessments: Is current practice state of the art? *Journal of Applied Behavior Analysis, 24*, 189–204. https://doi.org/10.1901/jaba.1991.24-189

Shook, A. C. (2012). A study of preservice educators' dispositions to change behavior management strategies. *Preventing School Failure: Alternative Education for Children and Youth, 56*, 129–136. https://doi.org/10.1080 /1045988X.2011.606440

Shukla, S., & Albin, R. (1996). Effects of extinction alone and extinction plus functional communication training on covariation of problem behaviors. *Journal of Applied Behavior Analysis, 29*, 565–568. http://dx.doi.org/10.1901/jaba.1996.29-565

Simonsen, B., Fairbanks, S., Briesch, A., Myers, D., & Sugai, G. (2008). Evidence-based practices in classroom management: Considerations for research to practice. *Education & Treatment of Children, 31*(3), 351–380. https://doi.org/10.1353/etc.0.0007

Singal, J. (2021). *The quick fix: Why fad psychology can't cure our social ills.* New York, NY: Farrar, Straus and Giroux.

Sullivan, A. L., Klingbeil, D. A., & Van Norman, E. R. (2013). Beyond behavior: Multilevel analysis of the influence of sociodemographics and school characteristics on students' risk of suspension. *School Psychology Review, 42*, 99–114. https://doi.org/10.1080/02796015.2013.12087493

Skinner, B. F. (1953). *Science and human behavior.* New York: Macmillan.

Skinner, C., Williams, R., & Neddenriep, C. (2004). Using interdependent group-oriented reinforcement to enhance academic performance in general education classrooms. *School Psychology Review, 33*, 384–397. https://doi.org/10.1080/02796015.2004.12086255

Slocum, T. A., Detrich, R., Wilczynski, S. M., Spencer, T. D., Lewis, T., & Wolfe, K. (2014). The evidence-based practice of applied behavior analysis. *The Behavior Analyst, 37*, 41–56. https://doi.org/10.1007/s40614-014-0005-2

Sugai, G., & Simonsen, B. (2012). *Positive behavioral interventions and supports: History, defining features, and misconceptions.* Center for Positive Behavioral Interventions and Supports. https://doi.org/10.1007/978-1-4614-6435-8_102148-1

Snider, V. E. (2006). *Myths and misconceptions of teaching: What really happens in the classroom.* Lanham, MD: Rowman & Littlefield Education.

Sprague, J., & Thomas, T. (1997). The effect of a neutralizing routine on problem behavior performance. *Journal of Behavioral Education, 7*, 325–334. https://doi.org/10.1023/A:1022827622948

Spriggs, A., Gast, D., & Ayres, K. (2007). Using picture activity schedule books to increase on-schedule and on-task behaviors. *Education and Training in Developmental Disabilities, 42*, 209–223. https://www.jstor.org/stable/23879996

Stage, S., & Quiroz, D. (1997). A meta-analysis of interventions to decrease disruptive classroom behavior in public education settings. *School Psychology Review, 26*, 333–368. https://doi.org/10.1080/02796015.1997.12085871

Stichter, J., Randolph, J., Kay, D., & Gage, N. (2009). The use of structural analysis to develop antecedent-based interventions for students with autism.

Journal of Autism and Developmental Disorders, 39, 883–896. https://doi
.org/10.1007/s10803-009-0693-8

Stockard, J., Wood, T. W., Coughlin, C., & Rasplica Khoury, C. (2018). The effectiveness of direct instruction curricula: A meta-analysis of a half century
of research. *Review of Educational Research, 88,* 479–507. https://doi.org
/10.3102%2F0034654317751919

Sugai, G. (2007). Prompting behavioral competence in schools: A commentary
on exemplary practices. *Psychology in the Schools, 44,* 113–118. https://doi
.org/10.1002/pits.20210

Sugai, G. (2008). Is PBIS evidence-based? *Presentation to the Illinois Leadership
Forum,* Rosemont, IL. Retrieved from http://www.pbis.org/common/pbis-
resources/presentations/0808sgpbisevidencebased_IL.ppt

Sugai, G., & Horner, R. (2002). The evolution of discipline practices: School-
wide positive behavior supports. *Child & Family Behavior Therapy, 24,*
23–50. https://doi.org/10.1300/J019v24n01_03

Sugai, G., & Horner, R. (2008). What we know and need to know about preventing problem behavior in schools. *Exceptionality, 16,* 67–77. https://doi.org
/10.1080/09362830801981138

Sutherland, K., Wehby, J., & Copeland, S. (2000). Effect of varying rates of
behavior-specific praise on the on-task behavior of students with EBD.
Journal of Emotional and Behavioral Disorders, 8, 2–8. https://doi.org/10
.1177/106342660000800101

Therrien, W. J. (2004). Fluency and comprehension gains as a result of repeated
reading: A meta-analysis. *Remedial and Special Education, 25,* 252–261.
https://doi.org/10.1177%2F07419325040250040801

Tincani, M. (2007). Beyond consumer advocacy: Autism spectrum disorders,
effective instruction, and public schooling. *Intervention in School and
Clinic, 43,* 47–51. https://doi.org/10.1177/10534512070430010601

Tincani, M., Castrogiavanni, A., & Axelrod, S. (1999). A comparison of the
effectiveness of brief versus traditional functional analyses. *Research in
Developmental Disabilities, 20,* 327–338. https://doi.org/10.1016/S0891
-4222(99)00014-1

Tincani, M., & De Mers, M. (2016). Meta-analysis of single-case research design
studies on instructional pacing. *Behavior Modification, 40,* 799–824.
https://doi.org/10.1177/0145445516643488

Tincani, M., & Crozier, S. (2007). Comparing brief and extended wait-time during small group instruction for children with challenging behavior. *Journal
of Behavioral Education, 16,* 355–367. https://doi.org/10.1007/s10864-007
-9047-9

Tincani, M., Lorah, E. R., & Dowdy, A. (2018). *Functional behavioral assessment
for students with autism spectrum disorder.* Pro-Ed.

Tincani, M., Ernsbarger, S. C., Harrison, T. J., & Heward, W. L. (2005). The effects of fast and slow-paced teaching on participation, accuracy, and off-task behavior of children in the Language for Learning program. *Journal of Direct Instruction, 5*, 97–109.

Tincani, M., & Travers, J. (2018). Publishing single-case research design studies that do not demonstrate experimental control. *Remedial and Special Education, 39.* 118–128. https://doi.org/10.1177/0741932517697447

Tincani, M., & Twyman, J. S. (2016). *Enhancing student engagement through active student responding.* Philadelphia, PA: Center on Innovations in Learning. https://www.researchgate.net/publication/306551589 _Enhancing_Engagement_through_Active_Student_Response

Todd, A. W., Campbell, A. L., Meyer, G. G., & Horner, R. H. (2008). The effects of a targeted intervention to reduce problem behaviors: Elementary school implementation of check in—Check out. *Journal of Positive Behavior Interventions, 10*, 46–55. https://doi.org/10.1177/1098300707311369

Touchette, P. E., MacDonald, R. F., & Langer, S. N. (1985). A scatter plot for identifying stimulus control of challenging behavior. *Journal of applied behavior analysis, 18*, 343–351. https://doi.org/10.1901/jaba.1985.18-343

Townley-Cochran, D., Leaf, J. B., Leaf, R., Taubman, M., & McEachin, J. (2017). Comparing error correction procedures for children diagnosed with autism. *Education and Training in Autism and Developmental Disabilities, 52*, 91–101.

Trussell, R. P. (2008). Classroom universals to prevent problem behaviors. *Intervention in School and Clinic.* 43, 179–185. http://doi.org/10.1177 /1053451207311678

Vincent, C. G., Randall, C., Cartledge, G., Tobin, T. J., & Swain-Bradway, J. (2011). Toward a conceptual integration of cultural responsiveness and schoolwide positive behavior support. *Journal of Positive Behavior Interventions, 13*(4), 219–229. https://doi.org/10.1177/1098300711399765

Wannarka, R., & Ruhl, K. (2008). Seating arrangements that promote positive academic and behavioural outcomes: A review of empirical research. *Support for Learning, 23*(2), 89–93. https://doi.org/10.1111/j.1467-9604 .2008.00375.x

Waters, M., Lerman, D., & Hovanetz, A. (2009). Separate and combined effects of visual schedules and extinction plus differential reinforcement on problem behavior occasioned by transitions. *Journal of Applied Behavior Analysis, 42*, 309–313. https://doi.org/10.1901/jaba.2009.42-309

Wilcox, G., Fernandez Conde, C., & Kowbel, A. (2021). Using evidence-based practice and data-based decision making in inclusive education. *Education Sciences, 11*(3), 129. https://doi.org/10.3390/educsci11030129.

Wolfe, K., Pyle, D., Charlton, C. T., Sabey, C. V., Lund, E. M., & Ross, S. W. (2016). A systematic review of the empirical support for check-in check-out.

Journal of Positive Behavior Interventions, 18, 74–88. https://doi.org/10 .1177/1098300715595957

Wood, W. M., Fowler, C. H., Uphold, N., & Test, D. W. (2005). A review of self-determination interventions with individuals with severe disabilities. *Research and Practice for Persons with Severe Disabilities, 30*, 121–146. https://doi.org/10.2511/rpsd.30.3.121

Xin, Y., Grasso, E., Dipipi-Hoy, C., & Jitendra, A. (2005). The effects of purchasing skill instruction for individuals with developmental disabilities: A meta-analysis. *Exceptional Children, 71*, 379–400.

Zimmerman, K. N., Ledford, J. R., & Barton, E. E. (2017). Using visual activity schedules for young children with challenging behavior. *Journal of Early Intervention, 39*, 339–358. https://doi.org/10.1177/1053815117725693

About the Author

Matt Tincani is a Professor in the Department of Teaching and Learning at Temple University. He focuses on the application of behavioral principles to improve language, academics, and social skills of diverse students with and without disabilities. His scholarly interests include positive behavior support in school and community settings, scaling-up of behavioral interventions, and single-case designs. His most recent work has explored issues of publication bias in single-case research, where he has advocated for publishing studies that do not yield experimental effects. He has been appointed to the editorial boards of several prominent journals in the field of special education, in addition to serving as associate editor of the *Journal of Positive Behavior Interventions*. A board certified behavior analyst since 2000, he was previously coordinator of Temple's graduate program in applied behavior analysis, in addition to his longstanding affiliation with the special education program.